IRISH ARMY ORDERS OF BATTLE

1923-2004

ADRIAN J. ENGLISH

Published by
TIGER LILY PUBLICATIONS LLC

FOR

ORBAT.COM

2005

To the memory of my late wife, Madeleine,
Who encouraged me to write about matters military,
And to Ravi Rikhye (happily still with us), who kept up the pressure

First Published: 2005
© Adrian J. English

Library of Congress Cataloging in Publication Data

Irish Army Orders of Battle 1923-2004
1. Ireland (Republic). Army history
I English, Adrian J. *1939 ñ*

British Library Cataloguing Data:

English, Adrian J. *1939 ñ*
Irish Army Orders of Battle 1923-2004
1. Ireland (Republic). Army history
I Title

ISBN   0972029672

Series Editor
Robert Mcarthur
Orbat.com History Books
rmcarthur@cox.net

Useful URLs
www.orbat.com
www.tigerlilypublications.com

Contents

Introduction

The Irish Defence Forces celebrated their 80th anniversary as a formal military organization in 2004. Born in civil war, they have never been called upon to fight against an external enemy but have nevertheless established a formidable reputation in international peacekeeping, both under the auspices of the United Nations and more recently the Partnership for Peace. The Irish Army, Naval Service and Air Corps, although they maintain distinct identities, underlined by different uniforms and rank structures, form a single entity. This brief study however deals only with the Army of which it does not pretend to be a comprehensive history merely seeking to trace the sometimes bewildering changes in its organization and equipment by means of a series of tables and appendices, with linking explanatory text. In order to do so it is however necessary to understand something of the historical and political and economic background which shaped its development. In doing so it will be assumed that the majority of the readers of this short work will be non-Irish and unfamiliar with the course of Irish history.

Adrian J. English
Dublin
January 1, 2005

Chapter 1 Historical and Political Background

From the Norman invasion of 1169 onwards Ireland became, at least in theory, subject to the English Crown. English rule was not however effectively enforced until the reigns of Elizabeth I and James I. Thereafter political disturbances in England tended to spill over into Ireland which was involved in both the Civil War, in which the Parliamentarians under Oliver Cromwell overthrew the monarchy and the so-called ìGlorious Revolutionî which overthrew the Roman Catholic King James II and re-established a Protestant monarchy. This was followed by a ruthless persecution of Irelandís Roman Catholic majority, which was not alleviated until the Catholic Emancipation Act of 1829 and polarized the Roman Catholic and Protestant sections of the Irish population.

Encouraged by the American and French Revolutions, a major uprising, with some French military support, occurred in 1798 and was brutally suppressed. Partly as a result of this abortive revolt the Act of Union of 1801 abolished the Irish Parliament and Ireland became fully politically integrated with England, Scotland and Wales in the United Kingdom.

The overwhelming majority of the Irish were subsistence level tenant farmers, living on a diet in which the potato had an unusual prominence. Failures of the potato crop in the late 1840s provoked a widespread famine as a result of which the population fell by approximately 60%. A further abortive revolt occurred in 1848 but an eventually successful movement for land reform, which permitted tenant farmers to buy out their holdings, dominated the remainder of the century.

From 1870 onwards agitation for the repeal of the Act of Union dominated Irish politics. As the 20th century dawned, the British Government had agreed in principal to restore Home Rule to Ireland. This was however perceived by the Protestant majority in the northern province of Ulster as a threat to submerge their identity in an overwhelmingly Roman Catholic political entity, governed from Dublin. In response, an illegal paramilitary force, known as the Ulster Volunteers was formed in 1913 and equipped largely with small arms smuggled in from Germany. Faced with a threatened mutiny in support of the Ulster Volunteers by the 3rd Cavalry Division of the British Army, stationed at the enormous military complex in the Curragh of Kildare, approximately 30 miles south-west of Dublin, the Government took no measures to suppress either the Ulster Volunteers or the Irish Volunteers, a similar but pro-Home Rule force which had been formed in Dublin more or less simultaneously. At about the same time, a major confrontation between the incipient trade union movement and the employers resulted in a resounding victory for the latter after much hardship of the strikers and their families. To defend its interests, the Irish trade union movement then also raised its own paramilitary force, known as the ìCitizen Armyî.

The outbreak of World War I in 1914 provided a convenient excuse for the British Government to shelve plans for Irish Home Rule, which had already shown a potential for major conflict between the Ulster Protestants and the Roman Catholic majority in the remaining 80% of the country. The Home Rule movement consequently split, the majority agreeing with its leadership in whole-heartedly supporting the British war effort while a minority became convinced that Home Rule and ultimately full independence could only be achieved by force of arms.

As the fighting on the Western Front turned against the Allies the time appeared ripe for armed insurrection in Ireland by the Irish Volunteers who by this time numbered approximately 18,000. Easter Sunday, April 23rd 1916, which fortuitously coincided with further reverses for the Allied forces in France, was chosen as the date for the rising.

As a result of misunderstood orders and the chronic disagreements amongst the leadership which had dogged all previous Irish attempts to challenge British rule, the rising was largely confined to Dublin where a total of less than 1000 Volunteers and Citizen Army members, armed only with largely obsolete rifles and side-arms, managed to occupy key strategic points. For five days during which most of the centre of Dublin was destroyed by artillery fire this puny force managed to resist attacks by regular British military forces originally numbering over 6,000, equipped with machine-guns and supported by artillery and reinforced daily by sea from Britain. The end was inevitable and having suffered over 25% casualties, including 60 dead, the survivors surrendered unconditionally on April 29th.

In addition to the 132 troops killed and 397, wounded the abortive rising had caused about 300 civilian deaths and 2,000 wounded and appalling damage to property. Consequently, public support for the aims of the insurgents was scanty and condemnation widespread. The execution of 16 of the leaders, one of whom was so badly wounded as to be unable to stand and was shot tied to a chair, rapidly changed this situation despite the release of the surviving rank and file of the insurgents after only a few months of imprisonment. Unsuccessful efforts to impose military conscription on Ireland the following year, which was resisted equally by both Ulster ìloyalistsî and southern nationalists, completed the alienation of a population most of whom would have been content with the restoration of an Irish Parliament under the British Crown. This was underlined by the results of the General Election of 1918, which returned 73 Nationalist members to the British Parliament as against only 26 Unionists. Regarding this as a clear mandate from the Irish people, the Nationalist members proclaimed themselves to be the legitimate Irish Parliament and within a brief period had established a surprisingly effective covert parallel government, complete with its own law courts, whilst military opposition to British rule was resumed and intensified.

After two and a half years of savage guerrilla warfare, countered by vicious repression, costing the British military and security forces 561 dead and 989 wounded, whilst the insurgents suffered approximately 30% of this rate of casualties and innocent civilians probably more, both parties were amenable to a Truce as a preliminary to negotiations regarding Irelandís political future. This came into effect on July 11th, 1921. The following day, Eamon de Valera, the New York born last surviving leader of the 1916 Rising, who owed his escape from execution to his United States citizenship and had emerged as the political leader of the Irish nationalists, met British Prime Minister David Lloyd George for discussions in London. These proved inconclusive in the face of the apparently irreconcilable British demands that Ireland remain within the British Empire and the Irish demand for an independent all-Ireland Republic.

Negotiations, between the British Government and a revised Irish delegation, led by Michael Collins, the most brilliant of the guerrilla leaders, resumed on October 11th and a Treaty granting southern Ireland dominion status within the British Commonwealth but reserving naval and coastal defence as functions of the British Armed Forces and permitting six of the nine counties of Ulster, in which Protestants formed a majority of the population, to opt out of the new political arrangement, was signed on December 6th, 1921. Although falling far short of their requirements, the Irish delegation reluctantly accepted this diluted form of independence as preferable to the threatened alternative of the resumption of ì immediate and terrible warî.

The Treaty was ratified by D· il ..ireann, the Irish de facto Parliament, by a narrow margin of 64 votes to 57, on January 7th, 1922.

Despite the democratic mandate for the Treaty, hard-line Republicans believed that the Treaty negotiators had sold out the ideal of a totally independent all-Ireland Republic for something utterly inferior and unacceptable. Even as the new Provisional Government of the Irish Free State began to set up a new administration to fill the voids left by the impending departure of the British, die-hard Republican elements of the army began to take over military posts and other strategic positions throughout the country. Matters came to a head when Republican forces seized the Four Courts, the main courts of justice, in Dublin, on April 13th.

Despite repeated and escalating provocations by the Four Courts garrison, culminating in the kidnapping of the Deputy Commander-in-Chief of the new National Army, the Provisional Government still hesitated to initiate hostilities against its former comrades in arms. Following the assassination of Field Marshal Sir Henry Wilson, on June 22nd. The British Government however issued an ultimatum to the Irish Provisional Government to the effect that the occupation of the Four Courts was regarded as a violation of the Treaty and that if it was to permitted to continue British troops would dislodge the occupants. Accordingly, the Four Courts were surrounded by troops of the National Army, equipped with two 18 pounder guns borrowed from the British; an ultimatum was issued and rejected; and at 4 a.m. on June 28th an attack commenced and with it ten months of bloody civil war which were to leave some 4,000 dead, including the Commander-in-Chief of the National Army, General Michael Collins and polarize Irish politics for the next half century. The bitterness of the legacy of the Civil War was exacerbated by the execution, without trial, by the Provisional Government, of 77 captured Republican leaders ñ almost five times as many as the leaders of the 1916 Rising executed by the British.

Chapter 2 Growing Pains

The Provisional Government had estimated a regular army of 4,000 to 5,000 as sufficient for its requirements. The Civil War however occasioned a drastic reassessment of the situation and the strength of the National Army eventually reached 55,000.

As a conflict between a relatively well equipped and increasingly professional army which enjoyed the support of the majority of the civilian population and a poorly equipped rag-tag and numerically inferior guerrilla force, the outcome of the Civil War was never in doubt and although skirmishing was to continue until the end of May 1923 anything approaching conventional warfare had ceased by the end of the previous September.

Although it was supported by limited numbers of armoured vehicles, light artillery pieces and even aircraft and towards its end included such subsidiary services as the Work Corps, the Coastal Infantry and the Railway Protection and Maintenance Corps, the army which fought and won the Civil War was essentially an infantry force which at the conclusion of hostilities consisted of 68 battalions. Following the successful conclusion of the Civil War the organization of this Army as a truly professional conventional military force was of over-riding importance.

The Armoured Car Corps had already been established in September 1923 to co-ordinate the activities of the 13 Rolls Royce, 7 Peerless and 64 Lancia armoured cars which had been handed over by the British and which had operated on an ad hoc basis throughout the Civil War. An Army Medical Service even pre-dated this, having been set up in April 1922. However it was not until March 1923 that the nine 18 pounder field guns, which had been similarly employed in support of the infantry, were grouped together formally as the Artillery Corps. The formal organization of the Engineers, Signals and Military Police Corps also took place at this time although it was not until the next year that a Transport Corps was formally set up and supply and ordnance functions continued to be directly subordinate to the Quartermaster General.

The beginning of the formal existence of the Army was the enactment of the Temporary Provisions for the Defence of Saorst·t ..ireann (The Irish Free State) on August 3rd, 1923. At this time, the establishment of an infantry battalion was 20 officers, 72 NCOs and 405 other ranks, a total of 497, organized as a battalion staff and services, three rifle companies and a light machine-gun unit. The over all organizational structure of the Army, now divided into nine territorial Commands, was as shown in the following table:

Table 1 ñ Orbat 1923

ARMY HQ (Dublin)

> HQ Armoured Car Corps (*13 Rolls Royce, 7 Peerless & 64 Lancia armoured cars distributed throughout nine companies*)
> HQ Artillery Corps (*equipped with 6 x18 pdr MK II and 4 x 18 pdr MK I guns*)
> > 1st Field Battery
> HQ Army Corps of Engineers *(incorporating the existing Works Corps, Railway Protection, Repair and Maintenance Corps and the Salvage Corps)*
> > HQ Army Signal Corps
> > HQ Army Medical Corps
> > HQ Transport Corps (Dublin):
> > > Horse Transport Depot (Dublin)
> > > Mechanical Transport Depot (Gormanston)
> > HQ Corps of Military Police

DUBLIN COMMAND (HQ Dublin)

> Command Armoured Car Company
> Command Military Police Company
> Command Services
>
> 1st Infantry Battalion (Dublin)
> 8th Infantry Battalion (Dublin)
> 13th Infantry Battalion (Dublin)
> 16th Infantry Battalion (Mountjoy Jail, Dublin)
> 20th Infantry Battalion (Carlow)
> 21st Infantry Battalion (Clones)
> 24th Infantry Battalion (Tallaght)
> 33rd Infantry Battalion (Naas)
> 37th Infantry Battalion (Gormanston)
> 45th Infantry Battalion (Mullingar)
> 48th Infantry Battalion (Navan)
> 49th Infantry Battalion (Dundalk)
> 50th Infantry Battalion (Gorey)
> 53rd Infantry Battalion (Cavan) ñ *disbanded November 1923*
> 55th Infantry Battalion (Dublin)
> 56th Infantry Battalion (Dublin)
> 57th Infantry Battalion (Dublin)
> 58th Infantry Battalion (Dundalk)

Table 1 ñ Orbat 1923 [CONTINUED]

Athlone Command (HQ Athlone)

2nd Infantry Battalion (Roscrea)
5th Infantry Battalion (Athlone)
22nd Infantry Battalion (Boyle)
23rd Infantry Battalion (Longford)
51st Infantry Battalion (Maryboro)

Command Armoured Car Company
Command Military Police Company
Command Services

DONEGAL COMMAND (HQ Drumboe)

3rd Infantry Battalion (Drumboe)
35th Infantry Battalion (Sligo)
46th Infantry Battalion (Donegal)

Command Armoured Car Company
Command Military Police Company
Command Services

CLARERMORRIS COMMAND (HQ Claremorris)

4th Infantry Battalion (Galway)
26th Infantry Battalion (Claremorris) ñ *disbanded November 1923*
34th Infantry Battalion (Tuam)
44th Infantry Battalion (Westport)
52nd Infantry Battalion (Claremorris)

Command Armoured Car Company
Command Military Police Company
Command Services

LIMERICK COMMAND (HQ Limerick)

    7th Infantry Battalion (Limerick)
    11th Infantry Battalion (Nenagh)
    12th Infantry Battalion (Ennis)

Table 1 (continued)

18th Infantry Battalion (Tipperary)
28th Infantry Battalion (Gort)
31st Infantry Battalion (Newcastle)
39th Infantry Battalion (Charleville)

Command Armoured Car Company
Command Military Police Company
Command Services

KERRY COMMAND (HQ Tralee)

6th Infantry Battalion (Killarney)
9th Infantry Battalion (Cahirciveen)
17th Infantry Battalion (Kenmare)
19th Infantry Battalion (Castleisland)
27th Infantry Battalion (Tralee)

Command Armoured Car Company
Command Military Police Company
Command Services

WATERFORD COMMAND (HQ Waterford)

14th Infantry Battalion (Waterford)
25th Infantry Battalion (Clonmel)
36th Infantry Battalion (Templemore)
41st Infantry Battalion (Wexford) ñ *disbanded November 1923*
47th Infantry Battalion (Kilkenny)

Command Armoured Car Company
Command Military Police Company
Command Services

CORK COMMAND (HQ Cork)

10th Infantry Battalion (Cork)
15th Infantry Battalion (Bandon)
30th Infantry Battalion (Bantry)
32nd Infantry Battalion (Macroom)

38th Infantry Battalion (Kanturk)
40th Infantry Battalion (Fermoy)

Table 1 (continued)

42nd Infantry Battalion (Youghal)

Command Armoured Car Company
Command Military Police Company
Command Services

CURRAGH COMMAND (HQ Curragh Camp)

29th Garrison Infantry Battalion
43rd Garrison Infantry Battalion
54th Garrison Infantry Battalion
59th Reserve Infantry Battalion
60th Reserve Infantry Battalion ñ *disbanded November 1923*
61st Reserve Infantry Battalion
62nd Reserve Infantry Battalion
63rd Reserve Infantry Battalion
64th Reserve Infantry Battalion ñ *disbanded November 1923*
65th Reserve Infantry Battalion ñ *disbanded November 1923*

Command Armoured Car Company
Command Military Police Company
Command Services

As will be seen from the above, the post-war Army had already begun to contract and had lost six battalions by the end of 1923. Strength, which in March 1923 had stood at 3,600 officers and 44,575 other ranks (a total of 48,176) a year later had fallen to 1,241 officers and 15,141 other ranks, totalling 16,382.

Down-sizing was by no means painless and March 1924 saw a crisis when a rump of officers objecting to both the rate of demobilization and the political basis upon which compulsory retirement was decided staged the nearest thing to a mutiny which the Irish Army has seen. This was suppressed by the resolute action of the Army Command, backed by the loyalty of the overwhelming number of units, only one battalion (the 36th, which was promptly re-deployed) having supported the dissident officers.

14

The legal basis of the Armyís existence was consolidated by the Defence Forces (Organization) Order of July 31st, 1924. This reduced the number of territorial Commands to three, plus the Curragh Training Camp and slashed the total number of Infantry Battalions from 59 to 27, further organized into nine Brigades so that the Order of Battle now looked something like this:

Table 2 ñ Orbat 1924

Army HQ

HQ Artillery Corps

      1st Field Batteries (e*4 x 18 pdr Mk I or Mk II*)
      2nd Field Battery (*4 x 18 pdr Mk I or Mk II*)

HQ Army Corps of Engineers *(incorporating the Works Corps, Railway Protection, Repair
    and Maintenance Corps and the Salvage Corps)*

HQ Army Signal Corps
    Army HQ Signals Company

HQ Army Medical Corps
    Field Division
    Hospital Division
    St. Bricinís Military Hospital

HQ Transport Corps (Dublin)

      Horse Transport Depot (Dublin)
      Mechanical Transport Depot (Gormanston)

HQ Corps of Military Police
Army School of Music
No. 1 Army Band

EASTERN COMMAND (HQ Dublin)

      2nd Armoured Car Company (*8 Rolls Royce, Peerless & Lancia amd cars*)
      Eastern Command Signals Company
      Eastern Command Military Police Company
      Eastern Command Transport Company

      No. 5 Brigade (HQ Kilkenny)

         13th Infantry Battalion

14th Infantry Battalion
15th Infantry Battalion

Table 2 (continued)

No. 6 Brigade (Dublin)

16th Infantry Battalion
17th Infantry Battalion
18th Infantry Battalion

No. 7 Brigade (Dublin)

19th Infantry Battalion
20th Infantry Battalion
21st Infantry Battalion

SOUTHERN COMMAND (HQ Cork)

3rd Armoured Car Company (8 *Rolls Royce, Peerless & Lancia armoured cars*)
Southern Command Signal Company
Southern Command Military Police Company
Southern Command Transport Company
No. 2 Army Band

No. 3 Brigade (HQ Cork)

7th Infantry Battalion
8th Infantry Battalion
9th Infantry Battalion

No. 4 Brigade (HQ Limerick)

10th Infantry Battalion
11th Infantry Battalion
12th Infantry Battalion

Table 2 (continued)

WESTERN COMMAND (HQ Athlone)

    4th Armoured Car Company (8 *Rolls Royce, Peerless & Lancia armoured cars*)
    Western Command Signal Company
    Western Command Military Police Company
    Western Command Transport Company
    No. 4 Army Band

    No. 1 Brigade (HQ Ballyshannon):

        1st Infantry Battalion
        2nd Infantry Battalion
        3rd Infantry Battalion

    No. 2 Brigade (HQ Athlone)

        4th Infantry Battalion
        5th Infantry Battalion
        6th Infantry Battalion

    Curragh Training Camp

    No. 8 Brigade

        22nd Infantry Battalion
        23rd Infantry Battalion
        24th Infantry Battalion

    No. 9 Brigade

        25th Infantry Battalion
        26th Infantry Battalion
        27th Infantry Battalion

Table 2 (continued)

> HQ Armoured Car Corps
> 1st Armoured Car Company (*8 Rolls Royce, Peerless & Lancia armoured cars*)

HQ Artillery Corps (Kildare)

> 1st Field Artillery Battery (4 x 18 pdr *Mk II guns*)
> 2nd Field Artillery Battery (4 x 18 pdr *Mk I guns*)
>
> Curragh Command Signals Company
> Curragh Command Military Police Company
> Curragh Command Transport Company
> No. 3 Army Band
> The Military College

As will be seen, there was now a Military College, located at the Curragh, together with the depots and schools of most of the emerging arms and services and an Army School of Music had been established under the direction of two German officers, Colonel Fritz Brase and Captain Christian Saurzweig.

By 1925 the Army possessed a total of 42,500 rifles (of which however only 8,000 were serviceable), together with 205 Vickers medium and 797 Lewis light machine-guns. Although four 4.5 inch howitzers, to equip a third field battery, had been obtained during 1925 and the number of 18 pounder field pieces on hand was gradually brought up to 25 no further significant quantities of infantry weapons were acquired between 1925 and 1931.

Numbers continued to decrease to 15,838 by the middle of 1925; 15,522 a year later; and 11,572 by 1927. With downsizing, the number of Infantry Battalions had also decreased in number from 27 to 16 in 1927 when the orbat was as follows:

Table 3 ñ Orbat 1927

Army Hq

> HQ Army Corps of Engineers
> HQ Army Signal Corps
> Army HQ Signals Company

20

HQ Army Medical Corps

Table 3 ñ Orbat 1927

        Field Division
        Hospital Division
        St. Bricinís Military Hospital

HQ Transport Corps (Dublin)

        Horse Transport Depot (Dublin)
        Mechanical Transport Depot (Gormanston)

        HQ Corps of Military Police
        Army School of Music
        No. 1 Army Band
        Army School of Equitation

EASTERN COMMAND (HQ Dublin)

    5th Brigade (HQ Kilkenny)

        13th Infantry Battalion (Naas)
        14th Infantry Battalion (Kilkenny)
        15th Infantry Battalion (Gormanston)

    6th Brigade (HQ Dublin)

        2nd Infantry Battalion (Dublin).
        5th Infantry Battalion (Dublin)
        7th Infantry Battalion (Dublin).

SOUTHERN COMMAND (HQ Cork)

3rd Brigade (HQ Cork)

        11th Infantry Battalion (Fermoy)
        12th Infantry Battalion (Clonmel)
        16th Infantry Battalion (Cork)

4th Brigade (HQ Limerick):

        9th Infantry Battalion (Limerick)
        10th Infantry Battalion (Templemore)

Table 3 (continued)

WESTERN COMMAND (Athlone)

   1st Brigade (HQ Boyle)

         3rd Infantry Battalion (Boyle)
         4th Infantry Battalion (Longford)

   2nd Brigade (HQ Athlone)

         1st Infantry Battalion (Galway)
         6th Infantry Battalion (Athlone)

Curragh Training Camp

   8th Infantry Battalion

   Armoured Car Corps
   1st Armoured Car Company ñ *8 Rolls Royce, Peerless and Lancia armd cars*
   2nd Armoured Car Company ñ *8 Rolls Royce, Peerless and Lancia armd cars*
   3rd Armoured Car Company ñ *8 Rolls Royce, Peerless and Lancia armd cars*
   4th Armoured Car Company ñ *8 Rolls Royce, Peerless and Lancia armd cars*

   Artillery Corps (HQ Kildare)

         1st Field Battery ñ *equipped with four 18 pounder guns*
         2nd Field Battery ñ *equipped with four 18 pounder guns*
         3rd Field Battery ñ *equipped with four 4.5 inch howitzers*

         Curragh Command Signals Company
         Curragh Command Military Police Company
         Curragh Command Transport Company
         No. 3 Army Band
         The Military College

The original intention had been to allocate one unit of each of the supporting arms and services to each Command. The shortage of artillery equipment however determined that the three batteries that constituted this arm were concentrated at Kildare, in the Curragh area, as were now also the four companies of the Armoured Car Corps.

The symmetry of the original numbering system of the infantry battalions was rapidly destroyed by cross-postings, amalgamations and disbandments and the number of infantry battalions continued to decline, the 14th, 15th and 16th being stood down during 1928, followed by the 10th, 12th and 13th in January 1929, the 11th being amalgamated with the 8th, which in turn amalgamated with the 3rd to give a total of nine, so that half way through 1929 the now greatly slimmed-down Army was organized as follows:

Table 4 ñ Orbat 1929

ARMY HQ

      HQ Army Corps of Engineers
      HQ Army Signal Corps
      Army HQ Signals Company
      HQ Army Medical Corps

            Field Division
            Hospital Division
            St. Bricinís Military Hospital

      HQ Transport Corps (Dublin)

            Horse Transport Depot (Dublin)
            Mechanical Transport Depot (Gormanston)

      HQ Corps of Military Police
            Army School of Music
            No. 1 Army Band
            Army School of Equitation

EASTERN COMMAND (HQ Dublin)

      2nd Infantry Battalion (Dublin)
      5th Infantry Battalion (Dublin)
      7th Infantry Battalion (Dublin)

SOUTHERN COMMAND (HQ Cork)

      4th Infantry Battalion (Cork)
      8th Infantry Battalion (Limerick)

9th Infantry Battalion (Clonmel)

WESTERN COMMAND (HQ Athlone)

1st Infantry Battalion (Galway)
6th Infantry Battalion (Athlone)

CURRAGH TRAINING CAMP

3rd Infantry Battalion.
Armoured Car Corps

1st Armoured Car Company ñ *8 Rolls Royce, Peerless and Lancia armd cars*
2nd Armoured Car Company ñ *8 Rolls Royce, Peerless and Lancia armd cars*
3rd Armoured Car Company ñ *8 Rolls Royce, Peerless and Lancia armd cars*
4th Armoured Car Company ñ *8 Rolls Royce, Peerless and Lancia armd cars*

Artillery Corps (HQ Kildare):

1st Field Battery ñ *equipped with four 18 pounder guns*
2nd Field Battery ñ *equipped with four 18 pounder guns*
3rd Field Battery ñ *equipped with four 4.5 inch howitzers*

Curragh Command Signals Company
Curragh Command Military Police Company
Curragh Command Transport Company
No. 3 Army Band
The Military College

Although all vestiges of a peacetime Brigade organization had now vanished and despite extreme financial stringency, the Army had acquired its first tank, a unique ì one offî Vickers ì Medium Dî, during 1929 and two Vickers Carden-Loyd tankettes were on order. 1929 was, of course, the year of the Wall Street Crash and the international economic depression, which followed it so that by 1931 the number of infantry battalions had been further, reduced to five and manpower strength had dropped to approximately 5,300. That year however saw the introduction of the steel helmet ñ German World War I M1916 pattern but manufactured by Vickers of Great Britain, due to the limitations on German exports of defence materiel imposed by the Versailles Treaty, which was adopted after experiments with the French ì Adrianî pattern helmet in 1928.

Since the end of the Civil War the country had been governed by the successors of the Provisional Government whilst until 1927 the defeated Republicans disdained political involvement in what they continued to regard as an illegitimate State. Although some of the more extreme Republican elements continued to finance the non-existent ì Republicî by bank robbery and other acts of brigandage, in 1927, the more rational elements, still led by Eamon de Valera, decided to continue the struggle for an all-Ireland Republic by constitutional means, forming the Fianna F· il (Warriors of Destiny!) Party, which was successful in obtaining a parliamentary majority in the General Election of 1931.

Bearing in mind that the Army was the direct descendant and spiritual heir of the force which had won the Civil War, there were wide-spread fears that the military would stage a coup díetat to annul the results of the 1931 Elections and when the new government took office, the following year, many of its members carried side arms which were at best superficially concealed under their civilian clothing. Following its established tradition of carrying out the democratically expressed will of the electorate, the Army, which was still largely officered by its political opponents, however accepted the new Government without question and continued to serve it loyally throughout the 16 consecutive years during which it remained in power. At the time of the critical change of government in 1931-32 the Army was made up as follows:

Table 5 ñ Orbat 1931

ARMY HQ

HQ Army Corps of Engineers
HQ Army Signal Corps
Army HQ Signals Company
HQ Army Medical Corps:

>   Field Division
>   Hospital Division
>   St. Bricinís Military Hospital

>   HQ Supply & Transport Corps (Dublin):
>   HQ Corps of Military Police
>   Army School of Music
>   No. 1 Army Band
>   Army School of Equitation

EASTERN COMMAND (HQ Dublin)

2nd Infantry Battalion (Dublin)
5th Infantry Battalion (Dublin)
6th (Reserve) Battalion
7th (Reserve) Battalion
1st City of Dublin Volunteer Reserve Battalion
2nd Supply & Transport Company

Table 5 (continued)

SOUTHERN COMMAND (HQ Cork)

4th Infantry Battalion (Cork)
8th (Reserve) Battalion
9th (Reserve) Battalion
10th (Reserve) Battalion
1st Cork Volunteer Reserve Field Battery
3rd Supply & Transport Company

WESTERN COMMAND (HQ Athlone)

1st Infantry Battalion (Galway)
11th (Reserve) Battalion
12th (Reserve) Battalion
13th (Reserve) Battalion
14th (Reserve) Battalion
4th Supply & Transport Company

Curragh Training Camp

3rd Infantry Battalion (Curragh)

HQ Cavalry Corps

1st Armoured Squadron ñ *13 Rolls Royce & 4 Lancia armoured cars*
2nd Armoured Squadron (cadre) ñ *1 Vickers Medium ì Dî tank; seven Peerless & nine Lancia armoured cars*

HQ Artillery Corps (Kildare):

1ˢᵗ Field Artillery Brigade (on mobilization):

1ˢᵗ Field Battery *(equipped with four 18 pounder guns)*
2ⁿᵈ Field Battery *(equipped with four 18 pounder guns)*
3ʳᵈ Field Battery *(equipped with four 4.5 inch howitzers)*

Artillery Depot & School (Kildare):

Table 5 (continued)

1ˢᵗ A/A Artillery Battery (Cadre) *(equipped with four 3 inch A/A guns)*

1ˢᵗ Field Engineer Company
1ˢᵗ Maintenance Engineer Company
1ˢᵗ Signals Company
1ˢᵗ Supply & Transport Company
1ˢᵗ Hospital Company
1ˢᵗ Military Police Company
No. 3 Army Band
The Military College

It will be noted that although it still consisted of only three batteries, the Artillery Corps was now organized as a brigade on mobilization and had also formed the nucleus of an anti-aircraft battery with four British 20 cwt 3-inch guns. The Transport Corps also became the Supply & Transport Corps in 1931.

The Eucharistic Congress of 1932 allowed the Army to hone its ceremonial skills and a new Mounted Escort unit, known colloquially and semi-officially as the ìBlue Hussarsî, was formed on an ad hoc basis, mainly from personnel of the Artillery and the Supply and Transport Corps as the Armoured Car Corps, which was soon to become the Cavalry, had no horse mounted elements!

Despite the smooth transfer of power in 1932, the new Government remained somewhat suspicious of the Army and its ultimate loyalty. In 1934 a new Tactical and Territorial Organization of the Defence Forces (which still consisted of the Army and Air Corps, with no naval component) was published. The most striking feature of this was the establishment of a new volunteer reserve element that was organized in named but un-numbered Regiments, of which there were nine, as follows:

Table 6 ñ The Volunteer Force 1934

> Regiment of *ORIEL* (*covering Counties Louth, Meath & Monaghan*)
> Regiment of *LEINSTER* (*covering Counties Kildare, west Wicklow*
> *Wexford and Carlow*)
> Regiment of *DUBLIN* (*covering the City and County of Dublin, the Borough of*
> *un Laoghaire and east Wicklow*)
> Regiment of *ORMOND* (*re-named Regiment of OSSORY in 1935 and covering*
> *Counties Kilkenny, Waterford and Tipperary*)
> Regiment of *THOMOND* (*covering Counties Limerick and Clare*)
> Regiment of *CONNAUGHT* (*covering Counties Galway, Mayo and Roscommon*)
> Regiment of *BREFFNI* (*covering Counties Cavan, Longford,*
> *Leitrim and Sligo*)
> Regiment of *TIRCONNAIL* (*covering County Donegal*)
> Regiment of *UISNEACH* (*covering Counties Laois, Offaly and Westmeath*)

A tenth non-territorial unit, the Regiment of *PEARSE*, was established in December 1935 as an Officers Training Corps with units in Trinity College Dublin, University College Dublin, University College Cork, University College Galway and the College of Surgeons, Dublin.

Each territorial Regiment nominally consisted of up to five battalions, one or two each of first and second line Volunteers and a Depot Battalion of third line Volunteers). Divided unevenly amongst the Regiments were also four Armoured Squadrons (numbered 3rd to 6th inclusive); nineteen Cyclist Squadrons (numbered 2nd to 20th); seven ì Horseî Squadrons (in practice all but two bicycle-mounted and numbered 2nd to 8th); 24 Field Artillery Batteries (numbered 5th to 28th) and six Light Batteries (numbered 2nd to 7th) plus four Anti-Aircraft Artillery Batteries (2nd Medium and 2 to 4th Light) and five Supply and Transport Companies (numbered 1st to 5th). The Regiment of *PEARSE* was designated as an Anti-Aircraft Artillery unit on mobilization. For no apparent reason and with no effect on their organization or tactical employment, the five regular infantry battalions, whilst remaining dispersed throughout the country, were grouped together as the ì Regiment of Riflesî.

Wartime mobilization plans envisaged a force of four reinforced brigades, each consisting of three infantry battalions and an artillery brigade, with appropriate supporting services. Of these the 1st (with two Volunteer battalions) and the 3rd (incorporating a single battalion of Volunteers) were brought together for training in the Curragh and Southern Command, areas respectively, during 1937 and 1938.

Although cynics regarded the Volunteer Force as a Fianna F· il militia and it certainly attracted members from amongst people who would have had nothing to do with what they still regarded as the ìFree State Armyî, the Volunteers settled down as a fully integrated element of the Defence Forces. The five-battalion regimental organization had however been over-ambitious and few of the regiments managed to mobilize more than four battalions for annual training. By the late 1930s the entire Force had become reduced to five regiments and eight battalions ñ three of the Regiment of *DUBLIN*; two of the Regiment of *DESMOND*; and one each of the Regiments of *THOMOND*, *UISNEACH* and *CONNAUGHT* - the Regiments of *ORIEL*, *BREFFNI*, *LEINSTER* and *TIRCONNAIL* having disappeared as separate entities whilst the deployment of the surviving battalions was frequently at variance with their territorial titles.

During 1933 the Army had taken delivery of three more 18 pounder field guns, bringing the total to 28 and four 3.7 inch pack howitzers, the latter being formed into the 1st ìLightî Battery, a term which also covered the limited number of mortars then available. The following year, the Armoured Car Corps, which had now acquired ìHorsedî and Cyclist elements (both of which were in fact mounted on bicycles) became the Cavalry Corps and in 1934-35 a successful experiment in the re-use of the armour, armament and turrets of the seven obsolete Peerless armoured cars, mounted on Leyland Terrier 6 x 4 truck chassis, resulted in the local construction of four relatively modern medium armoured cars. Two superficially similar Landsverk L-180 armoured cars, the design of which would appear to have heavily influenced that of the Leylands, were ordered in 1937 and delivered early in 1938 to be followed by six more vehicles of this type in 1939. The delivery of a further five L-180s, to bring the 1st Armoured Squadron up to its full authorized establishment of 17 vehicles, was however prevented by the outbreak of World War II and these ended up in service with the Swedish Army on the island of Gotland. 1935-36 had also seen the delivery of two Swedish Landsverk L-60 light tanks, which were acquired in lieu of the two Carden-Loyd tankettes, the order for which had been cancelled. Unfortunately, ambitious plans for the construction, under licence, of additional L-60s at the Great Northern Railway Works, in Dundalk, came to nothing, as did plans for the manufacture of small arms and ammunition.

Total equipment on hand now included 42,500 rifles, 297 Vickers medium and 797 Lewis light machine-guns, 28 18 pounder field guns, four 4.5 inch and four 3.7 inch howitzers, plus four 3 inch anti-aircraft guns, in addition to three tanks (one Vickers and two Landsverk), twelve heavy (four Leyland and eight Landsverk) and thirteen light (Rolls-Royce) armoured cars.

In 1938 the Irish Government also gained control of the so-called ìTreaty Portsî resulting in the addition of six coast artillery forts and a company of Coast Artillery Engineers to the Armyís order of battle. Implicit in the return of the ports was the acquisition of responsibility for seaward defence but as yet the Defence Forces did not contain any naval component.

Since the Italian invasion of Abyssinia (Ethiopia) in 1934 the failure of the League of Nations as a peacekeeping entity had become increasingly apparent. This was emphasized by Nazi Germanyís annexation of Austria and its dismemberment of Czechoslovakia.

As the major nations of Europe plunged headlong towards open war, frantic attempts were made by the Irish Government to modernize and improve the equipment of its Defence Forces. The peacetime establishment was increased to 8,021 made up of 759 officers, 2,061 NCOs and 5,201 other ranks. These were backed, in theory, by a Reserve of 21,723. However when Germany invaded Poland, on September 1st 1939, the Irish Defence Forces remained unimpressive, the Army still numbering only 5,915 all ranks, with a reserve of 14,470, which included 9,525 members of the Volunteer Force and was organized as follows:

Table 7 ñ Orbat 1939 (early)

ARMY HQ (Dublin):

> The ì Blue Hussarsî Mounted Escort ñ *ad hoc unit, formed as required*
> > A/A Artillery Battalion ñ*4 x 3 inch, 2 x 3.7 inch &4 40 mm L/60 A/A guns*
> Survey Company Corps of Engineers
> Army HQ Signals Company
> St. Bricinís Military Hospital
> 2nd Hospital Company
> Army School of Music
> No. 1 Army Band
> Army School of Equitation

EASTERN COMMAND (HQ Dublin)

> 2nd Infantry Battalion (Dublin)
> 5th Infantry Battalion (Dublin)
> *6th DUBLIN Infantry Battalion Volunteer Force*
> *7th DUBLIN Infantry Battalion Volunteer Force*
> *11th DUBLIN Infantry Battalion Volunteer Force*
> 2nd Maintenance Engineer Company
> 2nd Signals Company
> 2nd Supply & Transport Company
> 2nd Hospital Company
> 2nd Military Police Company

SOUTHERN COMMAND (HQ Cork)

4th Infantry Battalion (Cork)
9th *DESMOND* Infantry Battalion Volunteer Force (Croon)
10th *UISNEACH* Infantry Battalion Volunteer Force (Templemore)
12th *DESMOND* Infantry Battalion Volunteer Force (Castleconell)
13th *CONNACHT* Infantry Battalion Volunteer Force (Cahir)

Coast Artillery

Fort Mitchel (Spike Island, Cork Harbour) - *2 x 6î & 4 x 18 pdr guns*
Fort Davis (Eastern entrance to Cork Harbour) - *two 9.2 inch, two 6 inch and four 12 pounder guns + two fixed torpedo tubes*
Fort Camden (Western entrance to Cork Harbour) - *two 9.2 inch, one 6 inch and two 18 pounders + two fixed torpedo tube*
Fort Templebreedy (SW of Fort Camden) ñ *2 x 9.2î , 2 X 6î , & 4 x 12 pdr guns*
Fort Bere Haven (Bere Island) ñ *2 x 9.2î , 6 x 6î , 2 x4.5î & 8 x 12 pdr guns*

Coast Defence Engineer Company (Fort Camden)
3rd Maintenance Engineer Company
3rd Signals Company
3rd Supply & Transport Company
3rd Military Police Company

WESTERN COMMAND (HQ Athlone)

1st Infantry Battalion (Galway)
8th THOMOND Infantry Battalion Volunteer Force (Athlone)

Coast Artillery

Fort Dunree (7 miles north of Buncrana) - *Two 6 inch guns*
Fort Lenan (Lough Swilly) - *Two 9.2 inch guns*

4th Supply & Transport Company (Athlone)
4th Military Police Company

Curragh Training Camp

3rd Infantry Battalion (Curragh)
HQ, Depot & School Cavalry Corps

1st Armoured Squadron (Curragh)
2nd Armoured Squadron (Cadre)(Curragh)
1st ìHorsedî Cavalry Squadron (Curragh)
1st Cyclist Squadron (Curragh)

HQ, Depot & School Artillery Corps (Kildare):

1st Light Battery *(equipped with four 3.7 inch pack howitzers)*

1st Field Artillery Brigade

1st Field Battery *(four 18 pounder guns)*
2nd Field Battery *(four 18 pounder guns)*
3rd Field Battery *(four 4.5 inch howitzers)*
4th Field Battery *(four 18 pounder guns)*

2nd (Reserve) Field Artillery Brigade:

5th Field Battery Volunteer Force (four 18 pounder guns)
6th Field Battery Volunteer Force (four 18 pounder guns)
7th Field Battery Volunteer Force (four 18 pounder guns)
8th Field Battery Volunteer Force (four 18 pounder guns)

HQ, Depot & School Army Corps of Engineers
    1st Field Engineer Company
    1st Maintenance Engineer Company
HQ, Depot & School Army Signal Corps
    1st Signals Company
HQ, Depot & School Supply & Transport Corps (Dublin):
    1st Supply & Transport Company
HQ, Depot & School Army Medical Corps:
    1st Hospital Company
HQ, Depot & School Corps of Military Police
    1st Military Police Company
Band of the Curragh Training Camp
Military College

Chapter 3 A Precarious Neutrality (1939-45)

Although determined on a policy of military neutrality, its rather reluctant status as a British Dominion notwithstanding (a status reduced to that of a pure formality by the new Constitution introduced by de Valera and ratified in 1937), the Irish Government reacted immediately to the German invasion of Poland by calling out the Army reserves on permanent service and the cancellation of all scheduled demobilizations of serving personnel.

By April 1940 manpower strength had increased to 1,256 officers and 15,900 other ranks to give a total of 17,156 with an equipment inventory which included 3 tanks, 25 armoured cars (of which 13 were completely obsolete), 29 18 pounder field guns, four 4.5 inch and four 3.7 inch howitzers. Two British 3.7 inch and four Swedish 40 mm anti-aircraft guns had by now joined the four 3 inch museum pieces in the sole anti-aircraft unit which now expanded to a nominal battalion with a headquarters, one medium and one (incomplete) light battery and was re-located to Dublin. The infantry were reasonably well equipped with 42,413 rifles; 36 sub-machineguns of various types (many of them confiscated from subversive groups); 478 Vickers medium and 906 assorted light machine-guns, of which the latter however were mainly obsolete Lewises of World War I vintage, only 103 of 226 Bren guns ordered in 1937 having been delivered. The Army was particularly deficient in anti-armour weapons having only 41 ineffectual Boyes anti-tank rifles and a single example of the British 2 pounder (40 mm) anti-tank gun. Mortars were also in extremely short supply, the inventory comprising 48 Brandt 81 mm and a single 60 mm piece.

Pre-war emergency planning had envisaged the formation of four mixed brigades from the units of the peacetime Army and by the mobilization of reserve personnel - one in each Command area and a fourth in the Curragh Training Camp, which was to be elevated to the status of a Command on mobilization. This was carried out during the second half of 1939 but proved unwieldy in the context of the existing manpower resources so that two of the brigades were demobilized during the so-called ìPhoney Warî.

As a neutral country, Irish defence plans had envisaged two basic scenarios: (a) a British invasion to regain access to the ìTreaty Portsî and (b) a German invasion, as a preliminary to an invasion of Britain from the west. The German invasion and occupation of Norway in May 1940, followed closely by the fall of France and the evacuation of the remains of the British Expeditionary Force, together with some of their French allies, from Dunkirk increased the perceived threat of a German invasion and to supplement the two mobilized brigades, a number of ìMobile Columnsî were formed. Loosely based on the tactical concepts which had been used to effect in the War of Independence against Britain, each of these consisted of one or two infantry companies, reinforced where possible, with mortars, a troop of armoured cars and either a troop or battery of artillery. By the second half of 1940 the Army was therefore organized as follows:

Table 8 ñ Orbat 1940 (late)

<u>Army HQ</u>

> Survey Company Corps of Engineers
> Army HQ Signals Company
> Field Forces Signals
> Army School of Equitation
> No. 1 Army Band

<u>Eastern Command</u>

> Command HQ
> A/A Battalion (Dublin)
> 2nd Engineer Maintenance Company (Dublin)
> 2nd Garrison Signals Company (Dublin)
> 2nd Garrison Ordnance Company (Dublin)
> 2nd Garrison Supply & Transport Company
> St. Bricinís Military Hospital
> > 2nd Hospital Company (Dublin)
> 2nd Garrison Company Military Police (Dublin)

> Command Reserve (Dublin)

> > 7th Infantry Battalion (-)
> > 11th Infantry Battalion (-)
> > Armoured Car Troop ñ *four armoured cars & one 81 mm mortar*

> I Mobile Column Eastern Command (North Dublin) *ñ one reinforced company with one 81 mm mortar*

> II Mobile Column Eastern Command (South Dublin)*ñ one reinforced company with one 81 mm mortar*

Table 8 (continued)

    2nd Brigade (Dublin)

        Bde. HQ (Dublin)
        2nd Infantry Battalion (Dublin)
        5th Infantry Battalion (Dublin)
        6th Infantry Battalion (Dublin)
        2nd Artillery Battalion (Dublin) ñ 7th, 10th & 11th Fld. Btys.
        2nd Field Engineer Company (Dublin)
        2nd Field Signals Company (Dublin)
        2nd Field Supply & Transport Company (Dublin)
        2nd Field Ambulance (Dublin)
        2nd Field Company Military Police (Dublin)

Southern Command

        Command HQ
        3rd Engineer Maintenance Company
        3rd Garrison Signals Company
        3rd Garrison Ordnance Company
        3rd Garrison Supply & Transport Company
        3rd Hospital Company
        3rd Garrison Company Military Police
        Band of the Southern Command

        Command Reserve (Cork):

        8th Infantry Battalion (-) + *three 81 mm mortars*
        Armoured Car Troopñ *four armoured cars*

        I Mobile Column Southern Command (Tralee) ñ *one reinforced company + two 81 mm mortars & one Secn. Field Arty with two 18-pounder guns*

        II Mobile Column Southern Command (Limerick) ñ *one reinforced company + two 81 mm mortars & one Secn. Field Arty. with two18 pounder guns*

Table 8 (continued)

III Mobile Column Southern Command (Templemore) ñ *one reinforced company* + two *81 mm mortars & one Secn. Field Arty. with two 18-pounder guns*

COAST ARTILLERY

Fort Mitchel (Spike Island, Cork Harbour) - *two 6 inch and four 18 pounder guns*
Fort Davis (Eastern entrance to Cork Harbour) - *two 9.2 inch, two 6 inch and four 12 pounder guns + two fixed torpedo tubes*
Fort Camden (Western entrance to Cork Harbour) - *two 9.2 inch, one 6 inch and two 18 pounders + two fixed torpedo tubes*
Fort Templebreedy (South-west of Fort Camden) - *two 9.2 inch, plus two 6 inch and four 12 pounder guns*
Fort Bere Haven (Bere Island) - *two 9.2 inch, six 6 inch, two 4.5 inch and eight 12 pounder guns*
Coast Defence Engineer Company (Fort Camden)

1st Brigade

Bde. HQ (Cork)
4th Infantry Battalion (Cork)
9th Infantry Battalion (Castleconell)

12th Infantry Battalion (Limerick)
1st Artillery Battalion ñ 1st, 2nd & 3rd Fld. Btys. (Cork)
1st Field Engineer Company (Cork)
1st Field Signals Company (Cork)
1st Field Supply & Transport Company (Cork)
1st Field Ambulance (Cork)
1st Field Company Military Police (Cork)

Western Command

Command HQ
4th Engineer Maintenance Company
4th Garrison Signals Company
4th Garrison Ordnance Company
4th Garrison Supply & Transport Company
4th Hospital Company

38

Table 8 (continued)

    4th Garrison Company Military Police
    Band of the Western Command

Command Reserve (Athlone)

    1st Infantry Battalion (-) (Galway) + *three 81 mm mortars*
    10th Infantry Battalion (-) (Sligo) + *three 81 mm mortars*
    13th Infantry Battalion (-) (Athlone) + *three 81 mm mortars*
    Armoured Car Troop – *four armoured cars*

    I Mobile Column Western Command (Galway) – *one reinforced company + two 81 mm mortars and the 5th Field Battery with four 18-pdr guns*
    II Mobile Column Western Command (Sligo) – *one reinforced company + Two 81 mm mortars and the 6th Field Battery with four 18-pdr guns*
    III Mobile Column Western Command (Athlone) – *one reinforced company + two 81 mm mortars and the 8th Field Battery with four guns*

COAST ARTILLERY

    Fort Dunree (7 miles north of Buncrana) - *Two 6 inch guns*
    Fort Lenan (Lough Swilly) - *Two 9.2 inch guns*

Curragh Training Camp

    Command HQ (Curragh Camp)
    HQ, Depot & School Army Signal Corps
    1st Maintenance Engineer Company
    1st Signals Company
    HQ, Depot & School Supply & Transport Corps (Dublin):
    1st Supply & Transport Company
    HQ, Depot & School Army Medical Corps:
    1st Hospital Company
    HQ, Depot & School Corps of Military Police
    1st Military Police Company
    Band of the Curragh Training Camp
    Military College

Table 8 (continued)

3rd Infantry Battalion + *two 81 mm mortars*
1st Motor Squadron ñ *two, later four armoured cars, 16 scout cars, 39 motorcycles & 3 Motorcycle combinations*
1st Light Battery *with four 3.7inch howitzers*
Secn. Engineers
Secn. Signals
Medical Corps Section

HQ, Depot & School Cavalry Corps:

1st Armoured Squadron (Curragh) ñ *Broken up and equipment divided between Mobile Columns and 1st Motor Sqn.*
2nd Armoured Squadron (Curragh) ñ *non operational*
1st Cyclist Squadron (Curragh)
2nd Cyclist Squadron (Curragh) ñ *former 1st Horsed Squadron*

HQ, Depot & School Artillery Corps (Kildare):

7th Field Battery
9th Field Battery
10th Field Battery
11th Field Battery

HQ, Depot & School Army Corps of Engineers
1st Field Engineer Company

It will be noted that the artillery elements of the two brigades were now organized as battalions of two or three batteries rather than brigades.

Although the Irish Government had declined a German offer of large quantities of captured British materiel, all compatible with equipment in use, including 10,000 rifles, 550 machine-guns, 46 Field guns and 1,000 anti-tank rifles, mainly due to the near-impossibility of transporting it from the European mainland to Ireland, the mobilization of additional personnel, including 13 reserve rifle battalions and the receipt of additional equipment from Britain during 1941, which included four additional 18 pounder guns, four 4.5 inch howitzers, five additional 3.7 inch A/A guns, 30 Vickers medium plus

150 Bren and 200 Hotchkiss light machine-guns, in addition to 100 examples of the nearly useless Boyes anti-tank rifle, permitted the formation of two additional brigades so that four such formations once more existed by the later part of 1941. To avoid confusion with British troops on the Border with Northern Ireland, uniforms, which apart from the German-style helmet adopted in 1931 had resembled those of a US ìDoughboyî of 1917, although in a dark grey-green colour, were changed to resemble a grey-green version of those of the British Army and the British style steel helmet now supplanted the German pattern, of which sufficient numbers to equip the expanded Army had never existed.

Despite the acquisition of 26 Mk I Universal Carriers (incorrectly referred to as ìBren Carriersî) from Britain in 1940, followed by 30 nearly useless Beaverette scout cars (ten Mk IIIs and 20 Mk IVs), the Irish Army remained seriously deficient in armoured fighting vehicles. In an attempt to remedy this, a light armoured car was constructed on a 2 x 4 Morris truck chassis during 1940. Although this experiment was unsuccessful, seven similar vehicles, constructed on Ford truck chassis, by the Great Southern Railway Works at Inchicore, Dublin, armoured with boiler plate and armed with a single turreted Hotchkiss machine-gun, formerly mounted on scrapped Peerless armoured cars, were deemed to be sufficiently successful to justify the construction of fourteen similar vehicles, by Thompsons of Carlow. Finally, another series of 21 improved vehicles, this time armed with a Vickers medium machine-gun, were completed by the GSR and with this additional equipment the two existing armoured squadrons were for the first time brought up to full establishment and a third such unit formed whilst the carriers formed a fourth armoured squadron and a new type of light reconnaissance unit, the Motor Squadron, equipped at first with two and later four armoured cars, 15 un-armoured ìscout carsî (which were in fact cut down 10 and 16 h.p. Ford trucks), 42 motorcycles (of which three had side-cars, mounting a light machine-gun), a saloon car, a radio van, an ambulance and four to eight supply trucks, began to make its appearance

The order of battle was now as follows:

Table 9 ñ Orbat 1941 (late)

Army HQ

       Survey Company Corps of Engineers
       Army HQ Signals Company
       Field Forces Signals
       Army School of Equitation
       No. 1 Army Band

Table 9 ñ Orbat 1941 (late)

EASTERN COMMAND

    Command HQ (Dublin)
14th Rifle Battalion (Dublin)
22nd Rifle Battalion (Collinstown)
3rd Cyclist Squadron (Dundalk)
4th Cyclist Squadron (Dundalk)
5th Cyclist Squadron (Navan)
6th Cyclist Squadron (Dublin)
A/A Battalion (Dublin) ñ *units dispersed around the metropolitan area*
2nd Engineer Maintenance Company (Dublin)
2nd Garrison Signals Company (Dublin)
2nd Garrison Ordnance Company (Dublin)
2nd Garrison Supply & Transport Company (Dublin)
St. Bricinís Military Hospital
2nd Hospital Company (Dublin)
2nd Garrison Company Military Police (Dublin)

2nd Brigade (Dublin)

    Brigade HQ (Dublin)
2nd Infantry Battalion (Dublin)
5th Infantry Battalion (Dublin)
6th Infantry Battalion (Dublin)
2nd Artillery Battalion (Dublin) ñ 7th & 10th Fld. Btys.
2nd Field Engineer Company (Dublin)
2nd Field Signals Company (Dublin)
2nd Field Supply & Transport Company (Dublin)
2nd Field Ambulance (Dublin)
2nd Field Company Military Police (Dublin)

SOUTHERN COMMAND

COMMAND UNITS

    8th Infantry Battalion (Rineanna)
15th Rifle Battalion (Tralee)
19th Rifle Battalion (Little Island)

Table 9 ñ Orbat 1941 (late)

21st Rifle Battalion (Youghal)
23rd Rifle Battalion (Ennis)
31st Rifle Battalion (Little Island)
1st Cyclist Squadron (Mallow)
2nd Cyclist Squadron (Bantry)
7th Cyclist Squadron (Cappoquin)
8th Cyclist Squadron (Whitegate)

COAST ARTILLERY

Fort Mitchel (Spike Island, Cork Harbour) - *two 6 inch and four 18 pounder guns*
Fort Davis (Eastern entrance to Cork Harbour) - *two 9.2 inch, two 6 inch and four 12 pounder guns + two fixed torpedo tubes*
Fort Camden (Western entrance to Cork Harbour) - *two 9.2 inch, one 6 inch and two 18 pounders + two fixed torpedo tubes*
Fort Templebreedy (South-west of Fort Camden) - *two 9.2 inch, plus two 6 inch and four 12 pounder guns*
Fort Bere Haven (Bere Island) - *two 9.2 inch, six 6 inch, two 4.5 inch and eight 12 pounder guns*
Coast Defence Engineers (Fort Camden)
3rd Engineer Maintenance Company (Cork)

GARRISON UNITS

3rd Garrison Signals Company (Cork)
3rd Garrison Ordnance Company (Cork)
3rd Garrison Supply & Transport Company (Cork)
3rd Hospital Company (Mallow)
3rd Garrison Company Military Police (Cork)
Band of the Southern Command (Cork)

1st Brigade

Brigade HQ (Cork)
4th Infantry Battalion (Cork)
9th Infantry Battalion (Castleconnel)
12th Infantry Battalion (Limerick)
1st Artillery Battalion ñ 1st, 2nd & 3rd Fld. Btys. (Cork)
1st Field Engineer Company (Cork)
1st Field Signals Company (Cork)

Table 9 ñ Orbat 1941 (late)

1st Field Supply & Transport Company (Cork)
1st Field Ambulance (Cork)
1st Field Company Military Police (Cork)

WESTERN COMMAND

Command HQ (Athlone)
17th Rifle Battalion (Mullingar)
20th Rifle Battalion (Longford)

COAST ARTILLERY

Fort Dunree (7 miles north of Buncrana) - *Two 6 inch guns*
Fort Lenan (Lough Swilly) - *Two 9.2 inch guns*

GARRISON UNITS

2nd Engineer Maintenance Company (Dublin)
4th Garrison Signals Company (Dublin)
4th Garrison Ordnance Company (Dublin)
4th Garrison Supply & Transport Company (Dublin)
4th Hospital Company (Dublin)
4th Garrison Company Military Police (Dublin)
Band of the Western Command

4th Brigade

Brigade HQ (Mullingar)
1st Infantry Battalion (Galway)
10th Infantry Battalion (Sligo)
13th Infantry Battalion (Athlone)
4th Artillery Battalion ñ 5th, 6th & 8th Fld. Btys (Mullingar)
4th Field Engineer Company (Mullingar)
4th Field Signals Company (Mullingar)
4th Field Supply & Transport Company
4th Field Ambulance (Mullingar)
4th Field Company Military Police

Table 9 ñ Orbat 1941 (continued)

CURRAGH COMMAND

Command HQ (Curragh Camp)
16th Rifle Battalion (Kilkenny)
24th Rifle Battalion (Curragh)
25th Rifle Battalion (Curragh)

HQ, DEPOT & SCHOOL CAVALRY CORPS (Curragh)

1st Armoured Squadron ñ *8 Landsverk L-180 & 4 Leyland armoured cars*
2nd Armoured Squadron ñ*13 Rolls-Royce & 4 Ford MK V armoured cars*
3rd Armoured Squadron ñ*7 Ford Mk IV & 10 Mk V armoured cars*
1st Carrier Squadron ñ*26 Universal Carriers*
6th Cyclist Squadron

OTHER

HQ, Depot & School Artillery Corps (Kildare):
HQ, Depot & School Army Corps of Engineers
    1st Field Engineer Company
    1st Maintenance Engineer Company
HQ, Depot & School Army Signal Corps
    1st Signals Company
HQ, Depot & School Supply & Transport Corps (Dublin):
    1st Supply & Transport Company
HQ, Depot & School Army Medical Corps:
    1st Hospital Company
HQ, Depot & School Corps of Military Police
    1st Military Police Company
Band of the Curragh Training Camp
Military College

3rd Brigade

       Brigade HQ
       3rd Infantry Battalion (Curragh)
       6th Infantry Battalion
       7th Infantry Battalion
       3rd Artillery Battalion ñ 4th, 9th & 12th Fld. Btys.
       3rd Field Engineer Company
       3rd Field Signals Company
       3rd Field Supply & Transport Company
       3rd Field Ambulance
       3rd Field Company Military Police

The 13 mobilized reserve battalions were initially purely rifle battalions, with four companies. As their state of training advanced, their fourth companies were converted to machine-gun companies, primarily equipped with the Vickers medium machine-gun. As will be noted, sufficient artillery was now on hand to give each brigade a full artillery battalion of three batteries and there was also a relative proliferation of cyclist squadrons. As their name indicates, the latter were extremely light units, primarily mounted on pedal cycles, with a few motorcycles and trucks. In the absence of anything better, they were however invaluable for light reconnaissance, screening and internal security.

A part-time Local Security Force (LSF) had been formed in 1940, primarily for internal security and under the supervision of the Police. By 1941 this force had developed both an armed and an unarmed element, the latter mainly concerned with civil defence functions. In 1941 the armed element, renamed Local Defence Force (LDF), was separated from the unarmed Local Security Force to constitute something analogous to the British Home Guard. Although its military potential was never significant, the LDF eventually numbered almost 100,000 who would have been incorporated into the Army had Ireland become a belligerent.

By the end of 1940s army manpower had increased to approximately 40,000 and as the mobilized rifle battalions were converted to fully trained infantry battalions, the formation of four additional brigades was mooted. Somewhat surprisingly, this proposal was not immediately implemented as likewise was not a proposal to super-impose four divisional headquarters on the four brigades so that theoretically each Command would dispose of a division of two brigades and supporting units. In the context of the perceived threat scenario it was decided to form two rather than four divisions and that each division would have three rather than two brigades, with a reserve brigade in the Curragh Command area and an eighth brigade for the defence of the air port at Rineanna and the Foynes sea-plane base, both situated near the mouth of the river Shannon. Three new brigades and the nucleus of a fourth existed by the second half of 1941 and six of the existing eight brigades had been grouped under two divisional headquarters.

The 1st Division, the mission of which was to resist a possible German invasion from the south, had its headquarters at Cork and grouped together the 1st, 3rd and 7th Brigades, with their respective HQs at Clonmel, Cork and Limerick and the incomplete 8th Brigade at Rineanna. For its part, the 2nd Division, tasked primarily with resisting a possible British invasion from the north, had its HQ at Maynooth and grouped together the 2nd and 6th Brigades, both concentrated in the greater Dublin area, plus the 4[th,] with its HQ at Mullingar. The 5th Brigade, with its HQ at Kilkenny, was subordinate to Curragh Command and formed the strategic reserve.

Lack of equipment determined that the divisions lacked the usual supporting units at HQ level ñ tank battalions, medium, A/T and A/A artillery and engineer units ñ and were effectively merely co-ordinating units for their subordinate infantry brigades. The latter were however reasonably well equipped, apart from a lack of anti-tank and anti-aircraft weapons and mortars.

Very extensive exercises, involving both divisions and all units of the Defence Forces, were carried out during August/September 1942 at which time total manpower strength of the Army stood at approximately 38,000. During the 1942 ì Manoeuvresî the three armoured car squadrons were experimentally grouped together with the carrier squadron as a regiment but this arrangement was found to be less than satisfactory and was subsequently abandoned although five more ì heavyî armoured cars, two equipped with Madsen 20 mm guns in Landsverk-type turrets, the remainder with Vickers 0.50 inch machine-guns, were locally built on Dodge 2 x 4 truck chassis.

The only other organizational changes of any note were (a) the breaking up of the Carrier Squadron and the dispersal of its equipment amongst the infantry battalions and its replacement with a third Armoured Squadron, equipped with Ford vehicles; (b) the creation of a fourth armoured squadron, equipped with Beaverettes; and (c) the grouping of the field artillery in regiments, each of three field and one A/A/ - A/T battery (which was not formed due to lack of equipment), all in 1943.

Small quantities of additional equipment were received from 1941 onwards. These included 19,997 Springfield M1903 rifles, in the non-standard calibre of 0.30 rather than the standard 0.303 inches and 12 Schneider M97 75 mm field guns, all received from the United States during 1941. Eight more 3.7 inch A/A guns, together with two 6 inch coastal pieces for a new fort at the mouth of the Shannon and a pair of 60 pounder guns were received from Britain the following year, as well as 200 more Universal Carriers (this time Mk IIs) which were distributed among the infantry battalions. In 1943/44 20 additional 4.5 inch howitzers, four more 3.7 inch and two 40 mm A/A guns were also supplied by the UK together with four more 60 pounders and six 2 pounder A/T guns. Finally, 50 3-inch mortars were received in 1944. For the remainder of the World War II period (known in Ireland as ìThe Emergencyî) the order of battle of the Irish Army was as below.

Table 10 - Orbat 1942-45

Army HQ

> Survey Company Corps of Engineers
> Army HQ Signals Company
> Field Forces Signals
> St. Bricinís Military Hospital
> Army School of Equitation
> No. 1 Army Band

I DIVISION

HQ I Division (Cork)
> 2nd Armoured Squadron (Templemore) ñ *Rolls Royce and Ford Armoured Cars*
> 3rd Armoured Squadron (Rineanna) ñ *Ford Mk VI Armoured Cars*
> 1st Cyclist Squadron (Mallow)
> 2nd Cyclist Squadron (Bantry)
> 7th Cyclist Squadron (Cappoquin)
> 8th Cyclist Squadron (Whitegate)
> 13thCyclist Squadron Cyclist Squadron (Tarbert)
> 14th Cyclist Squadron (Kinsale)
> Band of the I Division (Cork)

1st Brigade

> Bde. HQ (Clonmel)
> 10th Infantry Battalion (Templemore)
> 13th Infantry Battalion (Cahir)
> 21st Infantry Battalion (Youghal)
> 1st Motor Sqn. (Cappoquin) ñ *4 armoured cars, 16 scout cars, 39 motorcycles & 3 Motorcycle combinations*
> 1st Field Artillery Rgt. (Templemore) - 1st, 2nd & 21st Fld. Btys.
> 1st Field Engineer Company (Clonmel)
> 1st Field Signals Company (Clonmel)
> 1st Field Supply & Transport Company (Clonmel)
> 1st Field Ambulance (Clonmel)
> 1st Field Company Military Police (Clonmel)

Table 10 (continued)

3rd Brigade

    Brigade HQ (Cork)
    4th Infantry Battalion (Cork)
    19th Infantry Battalion (Fermoy)
    31st Infantry Battalion (Little Island)
    3rd Motor Sqn. (Bruree) ñ *4 armd, 16 scout cars; 39 motorcycles & 3 motorcycle combinations*
    3rd Field Artillery Rgt. (Fermoy) ñ 9th, 12th & 16th Fld. Btys.
    3rd Field Engineer Company (Cork)
    3rd Field Signals Company (Cork)
    3rd Field Supply & Transport Company (Cork)
    3rd Field Ambulance (Little Island)
    3rd Field Company Military Police (Cork)

7th Brigade

    Brigade HQ (Limerick)
    9th Infantry Battalion (Croome)
    12th Infantry Battalion (Castleconnel)
    15th Infantry Battalion (Tralee)
    7th Motor Sqn. (Foynes) ñ *four armoured cars, 16 scout cars, 39 motorcycles & 3 Motorcycle combinations*
    7th Field Artillery Rgt. (Limerick) ñ 3rd, 17th & 18th Fld. Btys.
    7th Field Engineer Company (Limerick)
    7th Field Signals Company (Limerick)
    7th Field Supply & Transport Company (Limerick)
    7th Field Ambulance (Listowel)
    7th Field Company Military Police (Limerick)

8th Brigade (incomplete)

    Brigade. HQ (Rineanna)
    23rd Infantry Battalion (Ennis)

II DIVISION

    Division. HQ (Maynooth)
    3rd Cyclist Squadron (Dundalk)

Table 10 (continued)

    4th Cyclist Squadron (Dundalk)
    5th Cyclist Squadron (Navan)
    6th Cyclist Squadron (Dublin)
    11th Cyclist Squadron (Cavan)
    Band of the II Division (Maynooth)

2nd Brigade

    Brigade. HQ (Dublin)
    2nd Infantry Battalion (Dublin)
    5th Infantry Battalion (Bray)
    11th Infantry Battalion (Dublin)
    2nd Motor Sqn. (Dunboyne) ñ *four armoured cars, 16 scout cars, 39 motorcycles &*
        3 Motorcycle combinations
    2nd Field Artillery Rgt. (Dublin) ñ 10th, 14th & 19th Fld. Btys.
    2nd Field Engineer Company (Dublin)
    2nd Field Signals Company (Dublin)
    2nd Field Supply & Transport Company
    2nd Field Ambulance (Dublin)
    2nd Field Company Military Police (Dublin)

4th Brigade

    Brigade. HQ (Mullingar)
    6th Infantry Battalion (Mullingar)
    8th Infantry Battalion (Longford)
    20th Infantry Battalion (Athlone)
    4th Motor Sqn. (Boyle) ñ *four armoured cars, 16 scout cars, 39 motorcycles &*
        3 Motorcycle combinations
    4th Field Artillery Rgt. (Mullingar) ñ 8th, 15th & 20th Fld. Btys.
    4th Field Engineer Company (Mullingar)
    4th Field Signals Company (Longford)
    4th Field Supply & Transport Company (Mullingar)
    4th Field Ambulance (Mullingar)
    4th Field Company Military Police (Mullingar)

Table 10 (continued)

6th Brigade

Brigade. HQ (Dublin)
7th Infantry Battalion (Maynooth)
22nd Infantry Battalion (Collinstown)
6th Motor Sqn.(Clondalkin) *ñ four armoured cars, 16 scout cars, 39
    motorcycles & 3 Motorcycle combinations*
6th Field Artillery Rgt. (Dublin) ñ 5th, 6th & 11th Fld. Btys.
6th Field Engineer Company (Gormanston)
6th Field Signals Company (Dublin)
6th Field Supply & Transport Company (Dublin)
6th Field Ambulance (Dublin)
6th Field Company Military Police (Dublin)

EASTERN COMMAND

HQ (Dublin)
14th Infantry Battalion
A/A Battalion

GARRISON UNITS

2nd Maintenance Engineer Company
2nd Garrison Signals Company
2nd Garrison Ordnance Company
2nd Garrison Supply & Transport Company
2nd Transport Company
Horse Transport Company
2nd Hospital Company
5th Hospital Company
2nd Garrison Company Military Police
2nd Barracks Staff Detachment
3rd Battalion Construction Corps

SOUTHERN COMMAND

HQ (Cork)
14th Infantry Battalion

COAST DEFENCE ARTILLERY:

Fort Mitchel (Spike Island, Cork Harbour) - *2 x 6 inch and 4 x 18 pounder guns*
Fort Davis (Eastern entrance to Cork Harbour) - *two 9.2 inch, two 6 inch and four*

12 pounder guns + two fixed torpedo tubes
Fort Camden (Western entrance to Cork Harbour) - *two 9.2 inch, one 6 inch and*

two 18 pounders + two fixed torpedo tubes
Fort Templebreedy (South-west of Fort Camden) - *two 9.2 inch, plus two 6 inch*

and four 12 pounder guns

Fort Bere Haven (Bere Island) - *two 9.2 inch, six 6 inch, two 4.5 inch and eight 12 pounder guns*

Fort Shannon (Tarbert, County Kerry) - *two 6-inch guns*

Coast Defence Engineers

3rd Maintenance Engineer Company (Cork)
3rd Garrison Signals Company (Cork)
3rd Garrison Ordnance Company (Cork)
3rd Garrison Supply & Transport Company (Cork)
2nd Hospital Company (Mallow)
3rd Hospital Company (Cork)
2nd Garrison Company Military Police (Cork)

WESTERN COMMAND

HQ (Athlone)
1st Infantry Battalion (Galway)
17th Infantry Battalion (Letterkenny)
12th Cyclist Squadron (Sligo)
22nd Field Artillery Battery (Loughcutra Castle)

TABLE 10 (CONTINUED)

COAST ARTILLERY

Fort Dunree (7 miles north of Buncrana) - Two *6 inch guns*
Fort Lenan (Lough Swilly) - *Two 9.2 inch guns*

GARRISON UNITS

8th Field Engineer Company (Athlone)
8th Field Signals Company (Athlone)
8th Field Ambulance (Athlone)
8th Field Company Military Police (Athlone)
4th Maintenance Engineer Company (Athlone)
4th Garrison Signals Company (Athlone)
4th Garrison Ordnance Company (Athlone)
4th Garrison Supply & Transport Company (Athlone)
4th Hospital Company (Galway)
4th Garrison Company Military Police (Athlone)
2nd Battalion Construction Corps

CURRAGH COMMAND

HQ (Curragh)
24th Infantry Battalion (Curragh)
1st Armoured Squadron (Curragh) ñ *equipped with eight Landsverk L-180, four*
Leyland and five Dodge Armoured Cars
4th Armoured Squadron (Curragh) ñ *equipped with Beaverette Armoured Scout*
Cars
9th Cyclist Company (Curragh)
10th Cyclist Squadron (Port Laoise)

GARRISON UNITS

1st Maintenance Engineer Company (Curragh)
1st Garrison Signals Company (Curragh)
1st Garrison Ordnance Company (Curragh)

Table 10 (continued)

1st Garrison Supply & Transport Company (Curragh)
1st Transport Company (Curragh)
1st Hospital Company (Curragh)
1st Garrison Company Military Police (Curragh)
1st Internment Camp Staff (Curragh)
2nd Internment Camp Staff (Curragh)
1st Battalion Construction Corps (Curragh)
5th Battalion Construction Corps (Curragh)
HQ, Depot & School Cavalry Corps:
HQ, Depot & School Artillery Corps (Kildare):
HQ, Depot & School Army Corps of Engineers
      1st Field Engineer Company
      1st Maintenance Engineer Company
HQ, Depot & School Army Signal Corps
      1st Signals Company
HQ, Depot & School Supply & Transport Corps (Dublin):
      1st Supply & Transport Company
HQ, Depot & School Army Medical Corps:
      1st Hospital Company
HQ, Depot & School Corps of Military Police
      1st Military Police Company
Band of the Curragh Training Camp
Military College

5th Brigade

Brigade. HQ (Kilkenny)
3rd Infantry Battalion (Waterford)
16th Infantry Battalion (Kilkenny)
25th Infantry Battalion (Curragh)
5th Motor Sqn. (Flood Hall) ñ *four armoured cars, 16 scout cars, 39*
      motorcycles & 3 Motorcycle combinations
5th Field Artillery Rgt. (Kildare) ñ 4th, 7th & 13th Fld. Btys.
9th Field Engineer Company (Duncannon)
5th Field Signals Company (Kilkenny)
5th Field Supply & Transport Company (Kilkenny)
5th Field Ambulance (Kilkenny)
5th Field Company Military Police (Kilkenny)

A total of 56,502 served in the Army during the 1939-45 period, although not all simultaneously. The authorized War Establishment of 49,603 was however never filled and the actual strength in April 1945 was 37,786

The Irish Infantry Battalion had a manpower establishment of 881, organized in a Headquarters Company, three Rifle Companies and a Machine-gun Company. The latter was an unusually strong unit with an establishment of 16 Vickers medium machine-guns. In addition, each Rifle Company had (or was supposed to have) 12 light machine-guns, making a total of 36 for the battalion. Mortars were however in very short supply and for most of the wartime period the battalions averaged only two 81 mm Brandt mortars apiece although the receipt of 50 British 3 inch pieces in 1943-44 permitted the doubling of this allocation in the case of most battalions. Even more serious than the lack of mortars was that of anti-tank weapons, which was never satisfied. From 1943 onward most battalions also received nine Universal Carriers, one of which was used as transport for the battalion commanding officer, four for the mortar platoon and four for the reconnaissance platoon.

With only two light tanks, used for training purposes (the single medium tank was scrapped in 1940 and its 57 mm gun removed for us as an A/T weapon) Irish cavalry was entirely classifiable as ì lightî. The establishment of an Armoured Squadron was 114 with 17 armoured cars. In practice only the 1st Armoured Squadron, equipped with Leyland, Landsverk and eventually Dodge vehicles reached full establishment, the 2nd Squadron having 13 Rolls-Royces and the 3rd 14 Fords, the 4th having initially 26 Universal Carriers and later 30 Beaverette scout cars. The cavalry element of the brigade was the Motor Squadron, with an establishment of 163 and as already noted, an allocation of four armoured cars, 16 un-armoured scout cars, 39 motorcycles and three motorcycle combinations. The most numerous cavalry unit was the Cyclist Squadron with an establishment of 121 of whom three were mounted on motorcycles, the remaining 118 being mounted on pedal cycles. Apart from the rifles and side-arms carried by most of its members, this unit relied on three light machine-guns for fire support.

The basic unit of the Irish field artillery was the Battery of four pieces (4.5 or 3.7 inch howitzers or either 18 pounder or 75 mm guns). These were successively organized in (a) Brigades of three or four batteries; (b) Battalions of two or three batteries; and finally (c) Regiments with an HQ, three field and one anti-aircraft/anti-tank battery. The latter was largely a paper unit with machine-guns for A/A defence and only a single token 2 pounder A/T gun and even that only in the closing stages of the War. Manpower establishment of a Regiment was 456 all ranks. The anti-aircraft artillery was organized in a single Battalion with an ultimate strength of three medium and one light batteries (respectively equipped with British 3.7 inch and Swedish Bofors 40 mm A/A guns) plus four 3 inch and ten (naval) 12 pounder guns distributed in small detachments. The maximum manpower strength of this unit was about 1,000. There was no standard establishment for a Coast Artillery battery given the variation between the size and equipment of the various Forts.

The Engineer Field Company numbered 218 whilst the Maintenance Companies had only 25% of this number. The largest engineer unit was the Coast Defence Company with an establishment of 232 operating 17 searchlights whilst one of the smallest was the Ordnance Survey Company, with an establishment of 65.

Amongst other units the Field Supply and Transport Company had an establishment of 267, a Field Ambulance Company numbering 235 and a Military Police Field Company 62.

An element raised only during the wartime ìEmergencyî period was the Construction Corps, a non-combatant force, the organization of which varied between five battalions, two depots and finally ten companies of 244 each and which was demobilized in 1946.

Chapter 4 The Lean Years (1946-1959)

That Ireland had come through the 1939-45 war period with its neutrality intact was largely fortuitous. Despite the Trojan efforts which produced a well trained but ill-equipped army of almost 40,000, backed by an ill-trained and even worse equipped part-time Local Defence Force of 98,000; an extemporized naval force with six motor torpedo boats and a handful of auxiliary patrol craft; and an air arm with approximately 50 aircraft, less than half of which were of (largely obsolete) combat types, Irelandís military might was never an effective deterrent to aggression by either the Allies or the Axis.

A German invasion was never a serious possibility and although the Germans prepared comprehensive plans for the invasion and occupation of Ireland, these were based on incredibly defective intelligence, which included the false assumption of widespread support amongst the civilian population and, by a largely non-existent army of subversives. Although the successful German use of air-borne forces on a large scale in the invasions of Belgium and Crete caused an almost universal over-estimation of the potential of such forces, even had the Germans established a toe-hold in Ireland by an airborne landing, this could never have been sustained logistically in the face of British air and sea power. The few German agents landed in Ireland, either by air or from submarines, were rapidly captured whilst 600 members of the subversive ì armyî upon which they placed such high hopes of support, were rounded up and interned by the erstwhile extreme Republican Eamon de Valera who hanged six of them and permitted another three to starve themselves to death on hunger strike.

Any real danger of invasion would have come from the British (or later the combined British and US forces) from Northern Ireland to regain the use of southern Irish seaports and air bases. However, although the Irish Defence Forces would have been able to put up only a suicidal defence before being over-run, the British, at least, had recent memories of the difficulty of operating in the face of a largely hostile Irish civilian population and with the availability of base facilities in Northern Ireland, which also contained a substantial portion of the British defence industry, decided to forego the manifest advantages of bases in the South in the context of the predictable cost and the necessity of tying down an excessive proportion of their available manpower in maintaining security in the occupied territory. Thus, ironically, the partition of the island, which was so resented in the South and which had led to a bloody civil war, was the major factor in its being able to preserve its independence during World War II.

As a foot-note, it is interesting to remember that approximately 60,000 Irish men and women (7,000 of them deserters from the Irish Army) served in the Allied Armed Forces at one time or another during World War II whilst another 160,000 Irish civilian workers in Britain released a comparable number of British citizens for military service.

Even before Allied victory became a foregone conclusion the manpower strength of the Irish Army began to decline. In March 1943 it stood at 38,394; a year later it had dropped to 36,211; and by March 1945 it had fallen still further to 32,115.

Although the official State of Emergency was not revoked until September 1st 1946, plans for Irelandís post-war military establishment had been laid as early as February 1945. Having apparently learned little from the lessons of 1939, the manpower establishment of the post-war Irish Defence Forces, which however now included a small permanent naval element, was fixed at 12,740.

The peacetime Army, with a manpower establishment of 10,920, was to consist of the three pre-war territorial Commands ñ Eastern, Western and Southern, plus the training complex at the Curragh, with the status of a fourth Command. The main operational force was to comprise three Brigades, each organized essentially on the same lines as the brigades of the Emergency army although the infantry battalions were to be reduced to two active rifle companies. However, the mortar platoon, which was now a standard part of the infantry battalion establishment, was combined with the three machine-gun platoons in a Support Company. The peacetime manpower establishment of an infantry battalion was set at 23 officers, 88 NCOs and 424 other ranks to make a total of 535. The artillery regiments were likewise reduced to two field batteries although each of these was to consist of eight rather than four pieces. One armoured car squadron was to be retained at army level and an original proposal to establish four regimental cadres of anti-aircraft artillery (one in each of the territorial commands and one at Kildare as part of the Curragh training complex) was in practice reduced to a single A/A training regiment with two heavy and two light batteries. The composition of the peacetime Army therefore emerged as follows:

Table 11 ñ Orbat 1946-59

ARMY HQ

> The ìBlue Hussarsî Mounted Escort ñ *ad hoc unit formed as required*
> Army HQ Signals Company
> The Army School of Music
> No. 1 Army Band
> The School of Equitation

> EASTERN COMMAND (HQ Dublin)

> 2nd Engineer Maintenance Company
> 2nd Garrison Ordnance Company
> 2nd Garrison Supply & Transport Company

St. Bricinís Military Hospital
2nd Hospital Company
2nd Garrison Military Police Company

Table 11 (continued)

2nd Brigade (HQ Dublin)

2nd Infantry Battalion (Dublin)
5th Infantry Battalion (Dublin)
7th Infantry Battalion (Dublin)
2nd Motor Squadron (Dublin) *ñ equipped with six Ford Mk VI Armoured Cars, four Beaverette Scout Cars, eight Universal Carriers and soft-skinned vehicles*
2nd Field Artillery Regiment (Dublin) ñ *10th & 14th Fld. Btys. equipped with 16 25 pdr. Mk II gun-howitzers*
2nd Field Engineer Company (Cork)
2nd Field Signals Company (Cork)
2nd Supply and Transport Company (Cork)
2nd Field Medical Company (Cork)
2nd Field Military Police Company (Cork

SOUTHERN COMMAND (HQ Cork)

Coast Defence Artillery Southern Command:

Fort Mitchel (Spike Island, Cork Harbour) - *two 6 inch and four 18 pounder guns*
Fort Davis (Eastern entrance to Cork Harbour) - *two 9.2 inch, two 6 inch and four 12 pounder guns + two fixed torpedo tubes*
Fort Camden (Western entrance to Cork Harbour) - *two 9.2 inch, one 6 inch and two 18 pounders + two fixed torpedo tubes*
Fort Templebreedy (South-west of Fort Camden) - *two 9.2 inch, plus two 6 inch and four 12 pounder guns*   Fort Bere Haven (Bere Island) - two 9.2 inch, six 6 inch, two 4.5 inch and eight 12 pounder guns
Fort Shannon (Tarbert, County Kerry) - *two 6 inch guns* Coast Defence Engineers

1st Engineer Maintenance Company
1st Garrison Ordnance Company
1st Garrison Supply & Transport Company

Mallow Military Hospital
3rd Hospital Company
1st Garrison Military Police Company
The Band of the Southern Command

Table 11 (continued)

1st Brigade (HQ Cork)

4th Infantry Battalion (Cork)
12th Infantry Battalion (Limerick)
13th Infantry Battalion (Clonmel)
1st Motor Squadron (Fermoy) ñ *equipped with six Ford Mk VI Armoured Cars*
four Beaverette Scout Cars, eight Universal Carriers and soft-skinned vehicles
1st Field Artillery Regiment (Ballincollig) ñ *1st & 2nd Fld. Btys. equipped with 16 25 pdr. Mk II gun-howitzer*
1st Field Engineer Company (Cork)
1st Field Signals Company (Cork)
1st Supply and Transport Company (Cork)
1st Field Medical Company (Cork)
1st Field Military Police Company (Cork

WESTERN COMMAND (HQ Athlone)

Coast Defence Artillery Western Command:

Fort Dunree (7 miles north of Buncrana) - *Two 6 inch* *guns*
Fort Lenan (Lough Swilly) - *Two 9.2 inch guns*

4th Engineer Maintenance Company
4th Garrison Ordnance Company
4th Garrison Supply & Transport Company
Athlone Military Hospital
4th Hospital Company
4th Garrison Military Police Company
The Band of the Western Command

60

4th Brigade (HQ Athlone)

1st Infantry Battalion (Galway)
6th Infantry Battalion (Athlone)
4th Field Artillery Regiment (Mullingar) *ñ 8th & 15th Fld. Btys. Equipped*
with 16 25   pdr. Mk II gun-howitzers
4th Field Engineer Company (Athlone)
4th Field Signals Company (Athlone)
4th Field Supply and Transport Company (Athlone)
4th Field Medical Company (Athlone)
4th Field Military Police Company (Athlone)

Table 11 (continued)

CURRAGH TRAINING CAMP

3rd Infantry Battalion
1st Armoured Squadron ñ *equipped with eight Landsverk L-180, four*

Leyland

and five Dodge Armoured Cars plus four Beavertte Scout Cars
4th Motor Squadron ñ *equipped with six Ford Mk VI Armoured Cars*
plus four Beaverette Scout Cars, eight Universal Carriers and soft-skinned
vehicles
Anti-Aircraft Training Regiment (Kildare) ñ *equipped with 16 3.7 inch and*
four 40 mm L/60 A/A guns
1st Maintenance Engineer Company
1st Garrison Supply & Transport Company
1st Garrison Ordnance Company
1st Hospital Company
Military College
Depot & School Cavalry Corps
Depot & School Artillery Corps (Kildare)
Depot & School Corps of Engineers
Depot & School Signals Corps
Depot & School Supply & Transport Corps
Depot & School Ordnance Corps
Depot & School Corps of Military Police
Depot & School Medical Corps
Army Apprentice School ñ established 1956
General Military Hospital
1st Hospital Company
The Band of the Curragh Training Camp

It will be noted that one of the battalions of the 4th Brigade (3rd) was located at the Curragh as was the 4th Motor Squadron, which was also in theory part of the 4th Brigade.

In 1946 the part-time Local Defence Force was also re-organized and changed its name to Fûrsa Cosanta ¡ iti˙ il (FCA), which was merely the Irish translation of its original title. This force now consisted of 99 infantry battalions (only six of which, located in major urban areas, approached their full establishment strength whilst most approximated rather to companies than battalions) a motorized cavalry regiment, five field batteries, and single companies of engineers, signals, supply and transport and a field ambulance company.

Despite the availability of enormous quantities of war-surplus equipment, at bargain prices, acquisitions of new materiel remained parsimonious.

The more modern Lee-Enfield No. 4 replaced the old Lee-Enfield Mk III rifles, which had been the basic infantry weapon since the end of the Civil War, the Bren became the standard platoon support weapon and each rifle company now also included two to four 60 mm mortars for close support.
In 1948/49 four Churchill tanks were acquired to form a tank cadre although the position as regards armoured fighting vehicles remained so unsatisfactory generally that despite the re-engining of the Landsverk and Leyland armoured cars in the mid 1950s, the almost useless Beaverettes remained in service with cavalry units until ten years later.

The acquisition of the tanks was followed by that of 48 25 pounder Mk II gun-howitzers to re-equip the six regular field batteries; 12 17 pounder and six 6 pounder anti-tank guns; and an additional 18 Bofors L/60 A/A guns, to make a total of 24 weapons of this type.

The 1950s also saw the introduction of the Swedish Carl Gustav Kpist 45 as the Irish Armyís first standard sub-machinegun and at about the same time 72 Brandt M50A 120 mm heavy mortars (12 of which went to the 4th Artillery Regiment), two radar-controlled Bofors 40 mm L/70 A/A guns and quantities of Belgian Energa rifle grenades were also acquired.

In 1954 the establishment of the PDF infantry battalions underwent a minor change with the introduction of a Signals Section into the HQ Company and of an Assault Pioneer Platoon and an Anti-Tank Platoon to the Support Company. A proliferation of Universal carriers also permitted the allocation of this type of vehicle to be increased to 24 to 31 per battalion ñ one Mortar and two Machine-gun Platoons of seven vehicles each plus a section of three in the Assault Pioneer Platoon. Two Carriers were handed over to the Engineers and equipped experimentally with flamethrowers. The FCA infantry units, which had hitherto been armed solely with rifles, now also acquired Carl Gustav sub-machineguns and Bren light machine-guns whilst the sole FCA cavalry unit, the 11th Cavalry Regiment, in Dublin, received eight Ford Mk VI armoured cars. Despite the availability of 60 new 120 mm mortars, after the allocation of 12 to the 4th Field Artillery Regiment, the five FCA artillery batteries however had to make do with obsolete 18 pounder guns and 4.5 inch howitzers of which 37 and 38 respectively remained on inventory, the four 3.7 inch howitzers remaining in the Artillery School.

Chapter 5 From ì Integrationî to ì Dis-Integrationî (1959-79)

Poor pay and conditions (the pay of a private soldier was approximately US$1 a day during the mid 1950s) ensured that even the modest peacetime manpower establishment was never reached and the strength of the Army averaged about 8,000 throughout the late 1940s and most of the 1950s although some units, such as the 13th Infantry Battalion in the Southern Command, which for a period during the early 1950s fielded no less than FOUR rather than the usual two Rifle Companies, were actually over-establishment.

One victim of reduced manpower and a more puritanical concept of what was appropriate for a Republic (officially declared in 1949 with no other change in the countryís constitutional status) was the Mounted Escort which was abolished in 1948 by the austerity minded incoming Coalition Government which displaced de Valeraís Fianna F· il after 16 years continuously in office, ceremonial duties being taken over by first of all the 4th and from 1955 onward the 2nd Motor Squadron, which continues to perform them to this day.

Although neutrality, adopted pragmatically in 1939 and as we have seen sustained fortuitously throughout World War II, had become the corner-stone of Irish foreign policy, no serious effort was made to comply with the most basic requirement for the acceptance of neutral status under International Law: the maintenance of sufficient military forces to deny the use of the territory, coastal seas and air-space of the neutral state by one belligerent to the prejudice of the security of another.

As a result of a combination of a desire for greater government control of the part-time FCA, in the face of a revival of republican terrorist activity during the late 1950s and of an effort to create a semi-credible military force, on the cheap, in the context of falling numbers in the Permanent Defence Forces, a proposal for the integration of the regular army and the FCA was accepted by the Government in 1958. This involved the disbandment of two regular infantry battalions (the 7th in Dublin and rather ironically, the traditionally over-strength 13th in Clonmel) and the radical re-organization of the FCA to produce 17 infantry battalions, 3 motor squadrons, 3 field artillery regiments, 6 field and two A/A batteries, 3 engineer, 3 signals, 3 supply and transport, 3 medical and 3 military police companies for integration with regular elements to produce six brigades (two per Command) and five independent infantry battalions. Each of the six brigades was to have a single regular and two FCA infantry battalions, three of the brigades also having predominantly regular-manned tactical and logistic support elements whilst the other three had supporting units manned almost exclusively by FCA personnel, apart from a small regular training cadre. Integration was to be most complete in the case of the artillery, each of the three ì regularî artillery regiments having only one six-piece all-regular and two FCA batteries whilst the single A/A regiment also had one regular and two FCA batteries. The five independent FCA infantry battalions were to be divided between the Commands with two each in the Eastern and Southern Commands and a single battalion in the Western Command.

The acquisition of eight British Comet tanks during 1958-59 permitted the expansion of the existing tank cadre to a squadron which joined the 1st Armoured and 4th Motor Squadrons in the Curragh so that with one of each of the three types of cavalry unit now in existence a de facto training regiment could be assembled under command of the Cavalry Depot and School.

The new ì integratedî organization came into force on October 1st, 1959 when the order of battle of the Army was as follows:

Table 12 ñ Orbat 1959-73

ARMY HQ

Engineer Corps Survey Company (Dublin)
Army HQ Signals Company (Dublin)
Army Equitation School
No. 1 Army Band

EASTERN COMMAND (HQ Dublin)

20th Infantry Battalion FCA (Dublin)
21st Infantry Battalion FCA (Bray)
2nd A/A Artillery Battery FCA (Dublin) ñ *subordinate to 1st A/A Regiment; equipped with six 40 mm L/60 A/A guns*
2nd Engineer Maintenance Company
2nd Garrison Ordnance Company
2nd Garrison Supply & Transport Company
2nd Hospital Company (St. Bricinís Military Hospital Dublin)
2nd Garrison Military Police Company

2nd Brigade (HQ Dublin)

5th Infantry Battalion (Dublin)
7th Infantry Battalion FCA (Dublin)
8th Infantry Battalion FCA (Gormanston)
2nd Motor Squadron (Dublin) ñ *equipped with six Ford Mk VI Armoured Cars*

four Beavertte Scout Cars and soft-skinned vehicles
2nd Field Artillery Regiment (Dublin) ñ *10th PDF & 14th FCA Fld. & 19th FCA Hvy. Mrtr. Btys equipped with six 25-pdr gun-howitzers, six 18 pdr guns & eight 120 mm mrtrs.*
2nd Field Engineer Company (Dublin)
2nd Field Signals Company (Dublin)
2nd Supply and Transport Company (Dublin)
2nd Field Medical Company (Dublin)
2nd Field Military Police Company FCA (Dublin)

Table 12 (continued)

6th Brigade (HQ Dublin)

2nd Infantry Battalion (Dublin)
9th Infantry Battalion FCA (Kilkenny)
10th Infantry Battalion FCA (Wexford)
11th Motor Squadron FCA (Dublin) ñ *equipped with eight Ford Mk VI armoured cars*
6th Field Artillery Regiment FCA (Dublin) ñ *5th & 6th FCA Fld. & 11th FCA Hvy. Mrtr. Btys equipped with six 25-pdr gun-howitzers, six 18 pdr guns & eight 120 mm mrtrs.*
11th Field Engineer Company FCA (Dublin)
11th Field Signals Company FCA (Dublin)
11th Supply and Transport Company FCA (Dublin)
11th Field Medical Company FCA (Dublin)
6th Field Military Police Company FCA (Dublin)

SOUTHERN COMMAND (HQ Cork)

22nd Infantry Battalion FCA (Ennis)
23rd Infantry Battalion FCA (Cork)

Southern Command Coast Defence Artillery Cadre:

Fort Mitchel (Spike Island, Cork Harbour) - *two 6 inch and four 18 pounder guns*
Fort Davis (Eastern entrance to Cork Harbour) - *two 9.2 inch, two 6 inch and four 12 pounder guns + two fixed torpedo tubes*
Fort Camden (Western entrance to Cork Harbour) - *two 9.2 inch, one 6 inch and two 18 pounders + two fixed torpedo tubes*
Fort Templebreedy (South-west of Fort Camden) - *two 9.2 inch, plus two 6 inch*

and four 12 pounder guns   Fort Bere Haven (Bere Island) - two 9.2 inch, six 6 inch, two 4.5 inch and eight 12 pounder guns   Fort Shannon (Tarbert, County Kerry) - *two 6 inch guns* Coast Defence Engineers

3rd A/A Artillery Battery FCA (Limerick) - *subordinate to 1st A/A Regiment;*
> *equipped with six 40 mm L/60 A/A guns*
> 1st Engineer Maintenance Company
> 1st Garrison Ordnance Company
> 1st Garrison Supply & Transport Company

Table 12 (continued)

3rd Hospital Company
1st Garrison Military Police Company
Band of the Southern Command

1st Brigade (HQ Cork)

4th Infantry Battalion (Cork)
11th Infantry Battalion FCA
13th Infantry Battalion FCA
1st Motor Squadron (Fermoy) *ñ equipped with six Ford Mk VI Armoured Cars, four Beaverette Scout Cars and soft-skinned vehicles*
1st Field Artillery Regiment (Ballincollig) *ñ 1st PDF & 2nd FCA Fld. & 21st FCA Hvy. Mrtr. Btys equipped with six 25-pdr gun-howitzers, six 18 pdr guns & eight 120 mm mrtrs.*
1st Field Engineer Company (Cork)
1st Field Signals Company (Cork)
1st Supply and Transport Company (Cork)
1st Field Medical Company (Cork)
1st Field Military Police Company (Cork

3rd Brigade (HQ Limerick)

12th Infantry Battalion (Limerick & Clonmel)
14th Infantry Battalion FCA (Limerick)
15th Infantry Battalion FCA (Tralee)
3rd Motor Squadron FCA (Clonmel) *ñ equipped with three Beaverette Scout Cars and soft-skinned vehicles only*

3rd Field Artillery Regiment FCA (Templemore) ñ *9th & 12th FCA Fld. & 16th FCA Hvy. Mrtr. Btys equipped with six 25-pdr gun-howitzers, six 18 pdr guns & eight 120 mm mrtrs.*
3rd Field Engineer Company FCA (Limerick)
1st Field Signals Company FCA (Limerick)
1st Supply and Transport Company FCA (Limerick)
1st Field Medical Company FCA (Limerick)
1st Field Military Police Company FCA (Limerick)

Table 12 (continued)

WESTERN COMMAND (HQ Athlone)

24th Infantry Battalion FCA (Letterkenny)

Western Command Coast Artillery Cadre:

Fort Dunree (7 miles north of Buncrana) - *Two 6 inch guns*
Fort Lenan (Lough Swilly) - *Two 9.2 inch guns*

4th Engineer Maintenance Company
4th Garrison Ordnance Company
4th Garrison Supply & Transport Company
4th Garrison Military Police Company
Band of the Western Command

4th Brigade (HQ Athlone)

6th Infantry Battalion (Athlone)
16th Infantry Battalion FCA (Athlone)
17th Infantry Battalion FCA (Athlone)
4th Field Artillery Regiment (Mullingar) ñ *8th PDF Hvy. Mrtr. + 15th & 20th FCA Fld Btys equipped with six 25 pdr gun-howitzers, six 18 pdr guns & eight 120 mm mrtrs.*
4th Engineer Company (Athlone)
4th Field Signals Company (Athlone)
4th Field Supply and Transport Company (Athlone)
4th Field Medical Company (Athlone)
4th Field Military Police Company FCA (Athlone)

5th Brigade (HQ Galway)

1st Infantry Battalion (Galway)
18th Infantry Battalion FCA (Castlebar)
19th Infantry Battalion FCA (Boyle)
5th Motor Squadron FCA (Castlebar) ñ *equipped with three Beaverette Scout Cars and soft-skinned vehicles*
5th Field Artillery Regiment FCA (Galway) ñ *4th & 7th FCA Fld. & 13th FCA Hvy. Mrtr. Btys equipped with six 25-pdr gun-howitzers, six 18 pdr guns & eight 120 mm mrtrs.*
5th Engineer Company FCA (Galway)
5th Field Signals Company FCA (Sligo)
5th Field Supply and Transport Company FCA (Galway)
5th Field Medical Company FCA (Galway)

Table 12 (continued)

5th Field Military Police Company FCA (Galway)

CURRAGH TRAINING CAMP

3rd Infantry Battalion
1st Tank Squadron ñ *equipped with eight Comet and four Churchill tanks + eight Beaverette Scout Cars*
1st Armoured Squadron ñ *equipped with eight Landsverk L-180, Four Leyland and five Dodge armoured cars and four Beaverette Scout Cars*
4th Motor Squadron ñ *equipped with six Ford Mk VI Armoured cars, four Beaverettes and soft- skinned vehicles*
1st Air Defence Artillery Regiment (Cadre)(HQ & 1st Regular Battery, Kildare) ñ *equipped with six 40 mm L/60 A/A guns*
1st Maintenance Engineer Company
1st Garrison Supply & Transport Company
1st Garrison Ordnance Company
General Military Hospital
1st Hospital Company
Military College
Depot & School Cavalry Corps
Depot & School Artillery Corps (Kildare)
Depot & School Corps of Engineers
Depot & School Signals Corps
Depot & School Supply & Transport Corps
Depot & School Ordnance Corps

Depot & School Corps of Military Police
Depot & School Medical Corps

The Coast Defence Artillery installations in the Southern and Western Commands were both retained but these were now in a state of heavy preservation and were maintained by very small all-regular cadres of approximately a dozen in each case.

The FCA was now officially part of an integrated land defence force and although it seemed to have occurred to nobody in authority, the qualification ì ¡ iti˙ ilî (= ì Localî) in its official title, was now an anomaly and was to remain so. Although they still tended to inherit the cast-offs of their elders and betters in the Permanent Defence Force, the members of the FCA, at least theoretically, now had access to the whole gamut of weaponry and equipment on which they were supposed to train to the same level as the PDF. The stresses that this imposed on the members of a part-time force, who on an average drilled two nights a week and on Sunday mornings, with two weeks of full-time training each year, can only be imagined.

Numbers and morale in the permanent component of the Army continued to decline although salvation was to come from an unexpected quarter.

Ireland had finally become a member of the United Nations in December 1955, previous applications for membership having been vetoed by the Soviet Union and almost immediately began to participate in the peacekeeping operations of the UN.

In June 1958 a small number of officers was sent to Lebanon to join UNOGIL, the United Nations Observer Group in Lebanon, which was then rent by a civil war between the Moslem and Christian elements of its population. This group eventually expanded to 50 members.

The Lebanon operation lasted for less than five months before its members were transferred to UNTSO, the United Nations Truce Supervision Operation in the Middle East.

The operation which was to transform the Irish Defence Forces did not however occur until July 1960 when in response to the lapse of the newly independent Republic of Zaire, the former Belgian Congo, into total anarchy, followed by the secession of the mineral-rich province of Katanga, the United Nations Security Council requested the Irish Government to contribute a battalion to ONUC (Organization des Nations Units aux Congo).

Despite the depressed state of the Irish Defence Forces and their lamentable lack of modern equipment, the Government responded with alacrity, rushing through the necessary legislation to permit Irish troops to serve outside the State and on July

27th the first elements of the 689 man 32nd Battalion boarded US military transport aircraft, bound for central Africa. A few weeks later the 32nd Battalion was joined by the 706 man 33rd and for five months these two units formed the 9th (Irish) Brigade under the over-all umbrella of the UN force. In January 1961, as the 648 man 34th Battalion prepared to replace its two predecessors, Lieutenant General Se· n MacEoin, the Chief of Staff of the Irish Defence Forces, was appointed Force Commander of ONUC and continued to hold that appointment until the end of March the following year.

A total of 6,191 members of the Irish Defence Forces, of whom 26 lost their lives and 57 were wounded or injured, were to serve in 8 battalions, 2 infantry groups and 2 armoured car squadrons, under the UN, flag before the Congo operation ended in June 1964.

Although the members of the first Irish peacekeeping units went to tropical Africa sweltering in ì bulls woolî uniforms and otherwise equipped, apart from the Bren gun and the Carl Gustav SMG, to fight the Germans on the Western Front in 1914, the shortcomings in their equipment were rapidly made good. Tropical uniforms and more modern steel helmets were provided and major improvements occurred not only in the UN service units but the Army in general. The Belgian FN FAL rifle replaced the Lee Enfield, at least in the PDF elements of the ì integratedî Army, to be followed by the FN MAG machine-gun as a general-purpose replacement for both the Bren and the Vickers and the Swedish 84 mm Carl Gustav RCL, followed by the 90 mm Bofors Pv 1110, filled the long-standing need for effective anti-armour weapons at company and battalion level. Most importantly, combat experience on UN service improved both the training and morale of the participants to an unquantifiable degree.

The 337 man 2nd Infantry Group was still in the Congo when the Irish Government received a request for participation in another UN peacekeeping operation, this time in Cyprus where UNFICYP (UN Force in Cyprus) was attempting to keep the Greek and Turkish Cypriots from each otherís throats.

The 606 man 40th Battalion joined UNIFCYP in April 1964 and was followed by two more battalions ñ 41st and 42nd - and no less than nineteen infantry groups ñ 3rd to 13th and 18th to 25th inclusive - of from 130 to 537 members each, until October 1973 when the newly-arrived, company-strength 25th Infantry Group was transferred from Cyprus to UNEF, the United Nations Emergency Force in the Sinai Desert, in the immediate aftermath of the Yom Kippur War and its strength doubled to 262. In the tradition established by General MacEoin in the Congo, UNIFCYP was subsequently also to be commanded by an Irish officer, Major General James Quinn, who was appointed Force Commander in December 1976, an appointment that he continued to hold for over four years. Significant Irish participation in the Cyprus operation was completed by the 26th Infantry Group, which had followed its immediate predecessor to the Middle East before it was withdrawn prematurely in response to a deteriorating security situation at home in May 1974, by which time a total of 9220 Irish troops, of whom nine made the supreme sacrifice, had served in that troubled Mediterranean island. Although no further Irish units, as such, were to serve in Cyprus, another 234 members of the Irish Defence Forces had served there in various capacities up to October 1995.

From the point of view of improvements in equipment, the Cyprus operation was mainly beneficial to the long neglected cavalry arm of the Irish Army. The 2nd and 3rd Armoured Squadrons, of 96 and 89 men each, had gone to the Congo in October 1962 and April 1963 equipped with Irish-built Mk VI Ford armoured cars that were scarcely bulletproof at short range. Each squadron had 11 vehicles although armoured cars of this type had formed part of the 32nd to the 37th Battalions, inclusive, each of which had had an armoured car group of eight vehicles as part of its support elements. From November 1962 onwards the Congo Fords had been supplemented and finally supplanted by British built Ferret scout cars, provided by the UN. By now the dwindling number of Landsverk, Leyland and Ford armoured cars had clearly reached the end of their useful lives although they were to soldier on with the FCA cavalry squadrons into the mid 1970s and possible replacement vehicles were being actively studied. The French AML 245 was finally chosen although traditional parsimony dictated that these should be the mortar-armed H-60 version rather than the much more powerful H-90 which had a highly-effective 90 mm gun. The beginning of the Cyprus operation gave new immediacy to the purchase of the new vehicles and two were delivered to Ireland for training shortly after the departure of the 40th Battalion for Cyprus. Within a matter of weeks these vehicles were shipped to Cyprus where they were soon joined by six more. Another eight H-60s were acquired in August 1964 and shipped to Cyprus, the original eight vehicles being brought home with the 40th Battalion and four vehicles apiece were distributed to the 1st and 2nd Motor Squadrons.

In the meantime, events at home were beginning to overshadow the importance of UN peacekeeping activities.

With the eruption of violence in Northern Ireland, in the latter half of 1969, Irish troops were moved northward to the Border area where a number of ìfield hospitalsî (in fact dressing stations) were set up to receive the expected flow of injured refugees from Northern Ireland. Due to the acute under-manning of home service units (only the 4th and 12th Infantry Battalions approached their full establishment strength, with approximately 500 men each, whilst the remaining five regular battalions averaged only 100 men apiece) it was only possible to deploy four company-sized infantry groups ñ numbered 14th, 15th,

16th and 17th ñ to the border area and elements of the FCA had to be called into active service for ordinary day to day house-keeping and security duties in the rest of the country.

The deteriorating security situation, with the threat of an over-spill of violence from Northern Ireland into the Republic, particularly emphasized the Armyís deficiencies in motor transport and armoured fighting vehicles. Accordingly orders were placed in 1970 for another batch of 16 H-60s and a total of 20 H-90 armoured cars, together with 60 AML VTT M3 armoured personnel carriers of which four were command post variants. Delivery of the first instalments of this, the most formidable single order for AFVS ever placed by an Irish government (if we exclude the 200 Universal Carriers received in the 1940s) could not be expected until 1972 and as a measure of desperation 15 armoured scout cars, built on Unimog 4 x 4 truck chassis by Landsverk in Sweden for the defunct Belgian Congo Gendarmerie, and un-saleable following Congolese independence, were acquired as a stop-gap in 1971.

The first four H-90 armoured cars and 13 VTT APCs arrived about the middle of 1973 and were demonstrated to the media before being assigned to units. At about this time, Timoney Technology of Gibbstown, County Meath rolled out a prototype APC of original design of which five pre-production versions were ordered.

In September of that year the infantry groups on the Border were replaced by two new Infantry Battalions: the 27th, to be based in the Eastern Command area and cover the Border from Dundalk to Cavan and the 28th, to be based in the area of Western Command and cover the western portion of the border area. With the formation of these new units the peacetime establishment of the Army was increased to 13,026.

The last of the Churchill tanks had been withdrawn from service in 1970, followed by the Comets three years later and the Tank Squadron, which was anyway irrelevant in the prevailing security situation, was disbanded. In 1972 the 4th Motor Squadron was re-deployed from the Curragh to Longford, where it has remained. This left the Armyís orbat as follows:

Table 13 ñ Orbat 1973-77

ARMY HQ

Engineer Corps Survey Company (Dublin)
Army HQ Signals Company (Dublin)
Army Equitation School
No. 1 Army Band

Table 13 (continued)

EASTERN COMMAND (HQ Dublin)

20th Infantry Battalion FCA (Dublin)
21st Infantry Battalion FCA (Bray)
2nd Engineer Maintenance Company
2nd Garrison Ordnance Company
2nd Garrison Supply & Transport Company
2nd Hospital Company (St. Bricinís Military Hospital Dublin)
2nd Garrison Military Police Company

2nd Brigade (HQ Dublin)

5th Infantry Battalion (Dublin)
7th Infantry Battalion FCA (Dublin)
8th Infantry Battalion FCA (Gormanston)
27th Infantry Battalion (Dundalk) ñ *formed September 1973*
2nd Motor Squadron (Dublin) ñ *equipped with two AML H-90 and six H-60*
        armoured cars; four Unimog scout cars and four AML VTT APCs
2nd Field Artillery Regiment (Dublin)
        10th PDF & 14th FCA Fld. & 19th FCA Hvy. Mrtr. Btys *equipped with six*
        25 pdr gun-howitzers, six 18-pdr guns & eight 120 mm mrtrs.
2nd Field Engineer Company (Dublin)
2nd Field Signals Company (Dublin)
2nd Supply and Transport Company (Dublin)
2nd Field Medical Company (Dublin)
2nd Field Military Police Company FCA (Dublin)

6th Brigade (HQ Curragh)

2nd Infantry Battalion (Dublin)
9th Infantry Battalion FCA (Kilkenny)
10th Infantry Battalion FCA (Wexford)
11th Motor Squadron FCA (Dublin) ñ *equipped with five Landsverk L-180*
armoured cars + soft-skinned vehicles
6th Field Artillery Regiment FCA (Dublin)
        5th & 6th Fld. Btys. And 11th Hvy. Mrtr. Bty FCA *equipped with 12 25 pdr*
        Gun-howitzers & 6 AM50 120 mm mrtrs
11th Field Engineer Company FCA (Dublin)

74

Table 13 (continued)

11th Field Signals Company FCA (Dublin)
11th Supply and Transport Company FCA (Dublin)
11th Field Medical Company FCA (Dublin)
6th Field Military Police Company FCA (Dublin)

SOUTHERN COMMAND (HQ Cork)

22nd Infantry Battalion FCA (Ennis)
23rd Infantry Battalion FCA (Cork)
Coast Defence Artillery Cadre (Spike Island, Cork Harbour)
1st Engineer Maintenance Company
1st Garrison Ordnance Company
1st Garrison Supply & Transport Company
1st Hospital Company
1st Garrison Military Police Company

1st Brigade (HQ Cork)

4th Infantry Battalion (Cork)
11th Infantry Battalion FCA
13th Infantry Battalion FCA
1st Motor Squadron (Fermoy) ñ *equipped with two AML H-90 and six H-60
armoured cars; four Unimog scout cars and four AML VTT APCs*
1st Field Artillery Regiment (Ballincollig)
1st PDF & 2nd FCA Fld. & 21st FCA Hvy. Mrtr. Btys *equipped with six
25 pdr gun-howitzers, six 18 pdr guns & eight 120 mm mrtrs.*
1st Field Engineer Company (Cork)
1st Field Signals Company (Cork)
1st Supply and Transport Company (Cork)
1st Field Medical Company (Cork)
1st Field Military Police Company (Cork

3rd Brigade (HQ Limerick)

12th Infantry Battalion (Limerick & Clonmel)
14th Infantry Battalion FCA (Limerick)
15th Infantry Battalion FCA (Tralee)

Table 13 (continued)

3rd Motor Squadron FCA (Clonmel) *ñ equipped with three Landsverk L-180 armoured cars + soft-skinned vehicles*

3rd Field Artillery Regiment FCA (Templemore)
  9th Field Battery 6 x 25 pounder gun/howitzers
  12th Field Battery 6 x AM50 120mm Heavy Mortar
  16th Heavy Mortar Battery 6 x AM50 120 mm mrtrs

3rd Field Engineer Company FCA (Limerick)

1st Field Signals Company FCA (Limerick)

1st Supply and Transport Company FCA (Limerick)

1st Field Medical Company FCA (Limerick)

1st Field Military Police Company FCA (Limerick)

WESTERN COMMAND (HQ Athlone)

24th Infantry Battalion FCA (Letterkenny)

4th Engineer Maintenance Company

4th Garrison Ordnance Company

4th Garrison Supply & Transport Company

4th Hospital Company

4th Garrison Military Police Company

4th Brigade (HQ Athlone)

6th Infantry Battalion (Athlone)

16th Infantry Battalion FCA (Athlone)

17th Infantry Battalion FCA (Athlone)

28th Infantry Battalion (Finner Camp) *ñ formed September 1973*

4th Motor Squadron (Longford) ñ *two AML H-90, six H-60 armoured cars; four Unimog scout cars and four AML VTT APCs*

4th Field Artillery Regiment (Mullingar)

8th PDF Hvy. Mrtr. + 15th & 20th FCA Fld Btys *equipped with six 25 pdr gun-howitzers, six 18-pdr guns & eight 120 mm mrtrs.*

4th Engineer Company (Athlone)

4th Field Signals Company (Athlone)

4th Field Supply and Transport Company (Athlone)

Table 13 (continued)

4th Field Medical Company (Athlone)
4th Field Military Police Company FCA (Athlone)

5th Brigade (HQ Galway)

1st Infantry Battalion (Galway)
18th Infantry Battalion FCA (Castlebar)
19th Infantry Battalion FCA (Boyle)
5th Motor Squadron FCA (Castlebar) ñ *3 Leyland armd cars & soft-skinned vehicles*
5th Field Artillery Regiment FCA (Galway)
    4th Fld. Bty. 7th Fld. & 13th Hvy. Mrtr. Btys. *6 x 25 pdr; 12 x AM40 120mm*
5th Engineer Company FCA (Galway)
5th Field Signals Company FCA (Sligo)
5th Field Supply and Transport Company FCA (Galway)
5th Field Medical Company FCA (Galway)
5th Field Military Police Company FCA (Galway)

Curragh Training Ca mp

3rd Infantry Battalion
1st Armoured Squadron
1st Air Defence Artillery Regiment (Cadre)(HQ & 1st Regular Battery, Kildare; 2nd FCA Battery, Dublin; 3rd FCA Battery Limerick) ñ *18 40 mm L/60 A/A*
1st Armoured Squadron ñ 10 *AML H-90 armoured cars/3 Unimog scout cars*
1st Maintenance Engineer Company
1st Garrison Supply & Transport Company
1st Garrison Ordnance Company
1st Hospital Company
Military College
Depot & School Cavalry Corps
Depot & School Artillery Corps (Kildare)
Depot & School Corps of Engineers
Depot & School Signals Corps
Depot & School Supply & Transport Corps
Depot & School Ordnance Corps
Depot & School Corps of Military Police
Depot & School Medical Corps

General Military Hospital

It will be noted that Coast Artillery had now been reduced to a cadre in Cork Harbour. Although the Western Command installations were still maintained in a state of heavy preservation they were now the responsibility of the 4th Field Artillery Regiment, stationed at Mullingar.

Even though terrorist activity did not spill over from Northern Ireland into the Republic to the degree originally feared, the interception of several major attempts at gun-running by the Irish Navy, the discovery of illicit arms dumps and a series of bank robberies and kidnappings by Republican paramilitary groups and not least, the assassination of the British Ambassador, left little cause for complacence. In May 1974 the 26th Infantry Group was brought back from UN service in the Middle East, after only six weeks on station, when 32 People were killed and 174 injured by car bombs in Dublin and Monaghan. It was to be four years before another Irish unit could be spared for international peacekeeping.

With the tense security situation at home continuing, a third infantry battalion, the 29th, was activated in October 1976 and assumed responsibility for security along the central part of the Border in Cavan and Monaghan.

A year later another new infantry battalion, the 30th, was activated in Kilkenny, away from the Border area and this was combined with the existing 3rd Infantry Battalion and 1st Armoured squadron, both at the Curragh, to form the nucleus of a new 6th Brigade which also incorporated the 9th and 10th Infantry Battalions and the 6th Artillery Regiment (all FCA units from the existing 6th Brigade) and a new 3rd regular Field Battery (formed from elements of the Artillery School) plus the 6th Field Signals and 6th Supply & Transport Companies, both also new regular units. Of the ì orphanedî units of the existing 6th Brigade, the 2nd Infantry Battalion reverted to direct control by the HQ Eastern Command as did the 11th Cavalry Squadron, 11th Field Engineer, 11th Field Signals, 11th Supply & Transport, 11th Field Medical and both the 6th and 11th Field Military Police Companies. The Curragh Training Camp, which had always enjoyed the status of a separate functional Command, now became a new territorial Command with responsibility for the southeastern part of the country. The organizational structure of the Army was therefore now as follows as below.

Table 14 ñ Orbat 1977-79

Army Hq

      Engineer Corps Survey Company (Dublin)
      Army HQ Signals Company (Dublin)

78

Army School of Music

Table 14 (Continued)

No. 1 Army Band
Army Equitation School

EASTERN COMMAND (HQ Dublin)

Command HQ
2nd Infantry Battalion (Dublin)
20th Infantry Battalion FCA (Dublin)
21st Infantry Battalion FCA (Bray)
11th Motor Squadron FCA (Dublin) *ñ 5 Landsverk L-180, 4 AML H-60 armd cars, three Unimog scout cars*
2nd A/A Artillery Battery FCA (Dublin) *ñ equipped with six 40 mm L/60 A/A guns*
11th Field Engineer Company (Dublin)
2nd Engineer Maintenance Company
11th Supply and Transport Company (Dublin)
2nd Garrison Supply & Transport Company
2nd Garrison Ordnance Company
2nd Hospital Company (St. Bricinís Military Hospital Dublin)
11th Field Medical Company (Dublin)
6th Field Military Police Company FCA (Dublin)
2nd Garrison Military Police Company

2nd Brigade (HQ Dublin)

5th Infantry Battalion (Dublin)
7th Infantry Battalion FCA (Dublin)
8th Infantry Battalion FCA (Gormanston)
27th Infantry Battalion (Dundalk)
29th Infantry Battalion (Monaghan) *ñ from 1977*
2nd Motor Squadron (Dublin) *ñ 4 AML H-90, 6 H-60 Armd Cars, 3 AML VTT APC*
2nd Field Artillery Regiment (Dublin)
10th PDF & 14th FCA Fld. & 19th FCA Hvy. Mrtr. Btys *equipped with six 25 pdr gun-howitzers, six 18-pdr guns & 8 120 mm mortars.*
2nd Field Engineer Company (Dublin)
2nd Field Signals Company (Dublin)
11th Field Signals Company (Dublin)
2nd Supply and Transport Company (Dublin)

2nd Field Medical Company (Dublin)
2nd Field Military Police Company FCA (Dublin)

TABLE 14 (CONTINUED)

SOUTHERN COMMAND (HQ Cork)

    Command HQ
    22nd Infantry Battalion FCA (Ennis)
    23rd Infantry Battalion FCA (Cork)
    Coast Defence Artillery Cadre (Spike Island, Cork Harbour)
    3rd A/A Artillery Battery FCA (Limerick) *ñ equipped with six 40 mm l/60 A/A guns*
    1st Engineer Maintenance Company
    1st Garrison Ordnance Company
    1st Garrison Supply & Transport Company
    1st Hospital Company
    1st Garrison Military Police Company
    Band of the Southern Command

1st Brigade (HQ Cork)

    4th Infantry Battalion (Cork)
    11th Infantry Battalion FCA
    13th Infantry Battalion FCA
    1st Motor Squadron (Fermoy) *ñ3 AML H-90, 6 H-60 armd cars; 3 AML VTT APC*
    1st Field Artillery Regiment (Ballincollig)
        1st PDF & 2nd FCA Fld. & 21st FCA Hvy. Mrtr. Btys *equipped with six*
        25 pdr gun-howitzers, six 18-pdr guns & eight 120 mm mrtrs.
    1st Field Engineer Company (Cork)
    1st Field Signals Company (Cork)
    1st Supply and Transport Company (Cork)
    1st Field Medical Company (Cork)
    1st Field Military Police Company (Cork)

3rd Brigade (HQ Limerick)

    12th Infantry Battalion (Limerick & Clonmel)
    14th Infantry Battalion FCA (Limerick)
    15th Infantry Battalion FCA (Tralee)
    3rd Motor Squadron FCA (Clonmel) *ñ3 Landsverk L-180, 4 AML H-60 armd cars;*
        3 Unimog scout cars
    3rd Field Artillery Regiment FCA (Templemore) *ñ 9th Fld. Bty. equipped with six*

25 pdr gun-howitzers + 12th Fld. & 16th Hvy. Mrtr. Btys. Equipped with
12 AM50 120 mm mrtrs

3rd Field Engineer Company FCA (Limerick)

TABLE 14 (CONTINUED)

1st Field Signals Company FCA (Limerick)
    1st Supply and Transport Company FCA (Limerick)
    1st Field Medical Company FCA (Limerick)
    1st Field Military Police Company FCA (Limerick)

WESTERN COMMAND (HQ Athlone)

    Command HQ
    24th Infantry Battalion FCA (Letterkenny)
    4th Engineer Maintenance Company
    4th Garrison Ordnance Company
    4th Garrison Supply & Transport Company
    4th Hospital Company
    4th Garrison Military Police Company
    Band of the Western Command

4th Brigade (HQ Athlone)
    6th Infantry Battalion (Athlone)
    16th Infantry Battalion FCA (Athlone)
    17th Infantry Battalion FCA (Athlone)
    28th Infantry Battalion (Finner Camp)
    4th Motor Squadron (Longford) ñ equipped with four AML H-90 and six H-60
        armoured cars + three AML VTT APCs.
    4th Field Artillery Regiment (Mullingar)
        8th PDF Hvy. Mrtr. + 15th & 20th FCA Fld Btys equipped with six 25 pdr
        gun-howitzers, six 18-pdr guns & eight 120 mm mrtrs.
    4th Engineer Company (Athlone)
    4th Field Signals Company (Athlone)
    4th Field Supply and Transport Company (Athlone)
    4th Field Medical Company (Athlone)
    4th Field Military Police Company FCA (Athlone)

5th Brigade (HQ Galway)

    1st Infantry Battalion (Galway)
    18th Infantry Battalion FCA (Castlebar)
    19th Infantry Battalion FCA (Boyle)

5th Motor Squadron (Castlebar) ñ *3 Leyland armoured cars, 5 Unimog scout cars*
5th Field Artillery Regiment FCA (Galway)
    4th Field Battery *6 x 25 pdr gun/howitzers*
    7th Field Battery *6 x AM50 120mm Heavy Mortar*

TABLE 14 (CONTINUED)

    13th Heavy Mortar Battery *6 x AM50 120mm Heavy Mortars*
    gun-howitzers + 7th Fld. & 13th Hvy. Mrtr. Btys. Equipped with 12 AM50
    120 mm mrtrs.
5th Engineer Company FCA (Galway)
5th Field Signals Company FCA (Sligo)
5th Field Supply and Transport Company FCA (Galway)
5th Field Medical Company FCA (Galway)
5th Field Military Police Company FCA (Galway)

CURRAGH COMMAND (all units located at the Curragh except where otherwise stated)

    Command HQ
1st Air Defence Artillery Regiment (Cadre)(HQ & 1st Regular Battery, Kildare) ñ
    equipped with six RBS-70 SAM launchers and six 40 mm L/60 A/A guns
1st Maintenance Engineer Company
1st Garrison Supply & Transport Company
1st Garrison Ordnance Company
1st Hospital Company
Military College
Depot & School Cavalry Corps
Depot & School Artillery Corps (Kildare)
Depot & School Corps of Engineers
Depot & School Signals Corps
Depot & School Supply & Transport Corps
Depot & School Ordnance Corps
Depot & School Corps of Military Police
Depot & School Medical Corps
Army Apprentice School (Naas)
General Military Hospital
Band of the Southern Command

6th Brigade (HQ Curragh)

    3rd Infantry Battalion

30th Infantry Battalion (Kilkenny)
9th Infantry Battalion FCA (Kilkenny)
10th Infantry Battalion FCA (Wexford)
1st Armoured Squadron ñ *equipped with four AML H-90 and six H-60
armoured cars + three AML VTT APCs.*

TABLE 14 (CONTINUED)

3rd Independent Field Battery (Kildare) ñ*six 25 pdr gun-howitzers*
6th Field Artillery Regiment FCA (Kildare)
5th & 6th Fld. Btys., 11th Hvy. Mrtr. Bty FCA *12 x 25 pdr; 6 AM 50
120mm mortars*
6th Field Signal Company
6th Field Supply & Transport Company

Chapter 6 New Thinking on Defence (1979-2000)

By 1978 the security situation was considered to be sufficiently stable to permit the Irish Government to respond positively to a request for troops for a new UN peacekeeping operation in Lebanon. This country, with a delicately balanced population composed of almost equal parts Moslems and Maronite Christians, had lapsed into anarchy after Israel had established and equipped a surrogate military force, composed mainly of Lebanese Christians, to expel the Palestine Liberation Organization which had established itself in the country after its expulsion from Egypt and Jordan. Accordingly the 43rd Irish Battalion joined UNIFIL (United Nations Interim Force Lebanon) in April 1978. UNIFIL was to be Irelandís longest involvement in UN peace-keeping to date lasting for over 23 years with over 30,000 men and women serving in 47 battalions (43rd to 89th) until the 89th battalion completed its six-month tour of duty in November 2001. By a cruel coincidence, Irish fatalities during the Lebanon operation were also to total 47.

The UN service battalions, although each differed in detail, tended to follow the general organization of a home service battalion at full wartime establishment and thus usually numbered approximately 650 although there was considerable variation between individual units. The HQ Company however tended to add an ordnance and a military police element to the usual ì Aî and ì Qî Echelons (Administrative and Logistic Support Platoons), Signals, Transport and Medical Platoons and in the absence of a conventional Support Company, an Assault Pioneer Platoon was frequently also added to the HQ Company. There were invariably three Infantry Companies, each with a Weapons Platoon containing mortar, machine-gun, anti-armour and reconnaissance sections although the Company frequently contained two rather than the usual three Rifle Platoons. Instead of the conventional Support Company, each UN service battalion usually contained what was somewhat misleadingly termed a ì Reconnaissance Companyî. This almost invariably included a troop of four H-90 armoured cars; an APC support group, which was a purely î liftî unit with 14 Panhard (later ten Finnish SISU) APCs, which could be placed at the disposal of the Infantry Companies and Platoons as necessary; a heavy mortar platoon with four 120 mm mortars; and an anti-tank platoon, equipped with 90 mm RCLs. As the most heavily armed element of most of the national contingents the ì Reconnaissance Companyî of the Irish UN battalions frequently found itself being employed as the Force Mobile Reserve. The Infantry Groups were flexible units which normally approximated to a two-company battalion, without tactical support elements, but which sometimes amounted to no more than a reinforced company.

Irish officers continued to be in demand for senior appointments in UN peacekeeping operations and on February 5th, 1981 Lieutenant General William Callaghan was appointed Force Commander of UNIFCYP, an appointment that he would continue to hold until May 7th, 1986.

84

If the Irish Army was back in the peacekeeping business, time was running out for its ì integratedî organization. Although some units of the FCA had reached a surprisingly high degree of efficiency, it had always been unreasonable to expect the members of a part-time force to master the complexity of modern military equipment and match the efficiency of full-time professional soldiers and the integration of the FCA and PDF had been only partly successful. Also, with an effective training strength of only 15,000 out of a nominal 22,000 the FCA would have been inadequate to reinforce the PDF sufficiently to produce six full brigades on mobilization. The writing had been on the wall for the integrated arrangement since the formation of the new 6th Brigade and Curragh Command and accordingly the experiment officially came to an end on September 26th 1979 when the FCA was formally separated from the PDF and the number of brigades was reduced to four (each with two or three infantry battalions), plus an ì Infantry Forceî, in effect a two-battalion infantry brigade with no dedicated tactical or logistic support elements, in the border region of Eastern Command. The revised orbat of the Army therefore emerged as follows:

Table 15 ñ Orbat 1979 - 2000

ARMY HQ:

> Army HQ (Parkgate, Dublin)
> Engineer Survey Coy. (Phoenix Park, Dublin)
> Army HQ Signals Coy. (McKee Barracks, Dublin)
> 1st Garrison Coy. Military Police (Government Buildings, Dublin)

EASTERN COMMAND

> Command HQ (Collins Barracks, Dublin)
> McKee Barracks Coy. (McKee Barracks, Dublin)
> Clancy Barracks Coy. (Clancy Barracks Dublin)
> 2nd Engineer Maintenance Coy. (Collins Barracks, Dublin)
> Army Ordnance School (Dublin)
> 2nd Garrison Ordnance Coy. (Cathal Brugha Barracks, Dublin)
> 2nd Garrison Supply & Transport Coy. (McKee Barracks, Dublin)
> Base Workshops Coy. Supply & Transport Corps (Clancy Barracks, Dublin)
> 2nd Hospital Coy. (St. Bricinís Hospital, Dublin)
> St. Bricinís Hospital (Dublin)
> 2nd Garrison Coy. Military Police (Collins Barracks, Dublin)
> Army school of Music (Cathal Brugha Barracks, Dublin)
> No. 1 Army Band (Cathal Brugha Barracks, Dublin)
> Command Training Depot (Cathal Brugha Barracks, Dublin)

TABLE 15 (CONTINUED)

Equitation School (McKee Barracks, Dublin)
Army Catering School (McKee Barracks, Dublin)

2nd Infantry Brigade

Brigade HQ (Collins Barracks, Dublin)

2nd Infy. Bn. (Cathal Brugha Barracks, Dublin)

5th Infy. Bn. (Collins Barracks, Dublin) ñ *had 1 APC Coy., 12 AML VTT M3 APCs*
2nd Cav. Sqn. (Cathal Brugha Barracks, Dublin) - *equipped with four AML 245 H-*

90 and six AML 245 H-60 armoured cars plus three AML VTT M3 APCs
2nd Field Arty. Rgt (HQ, 10th & 18th Field Batteries - McKee Barracks, Dublin) -
equipped with twelve 25 pounder gun-howitzers
2nd Field Engineer Coy. (Clancy Barracks, Dublin)
2nd Field Signals Coy. (Collins Barracks, Dublin)
2nd Field Supply & Transport Coy. (Collins Barracks, Dublin)
2nd Field Med. Coy (FCA) (Cathal Brugha Barracks, Dublin) 2nd Field Coy
Military Police (FCA) (Collins Barracks, Dublin)

Eastern Command Infantry Force:

HQ (Gormanston, Co. Meath)

27th Infy. Bn. (HQ, HQ Coy & A Coy., Dundalk; B Coy. Gormanston; Spt. Coy.
Castleblaney)

29th Infy. Bn. (HQ, HQ Coy & Spt. Coy., Cootehill; A Coy. Monaghan; B Coy.
Cavan) - *had five Timoney Mk IV APCs*

Eastern Command FCA Group:
HQ (Cathal Brugha Barracks, Dublin) 7th Infy. Bn. (HQ & A & C Coys., McKee
Barracks, Dublin; B Coy. Swords; D Coy., Navan; E Coy., Kells)
8th Infy. Bn. (HQ & A Coy., Dundalk; B Coy. Drogheda; C Coy., Castleblaney; D
Coy. Cavan; E Coy., Balieboro)
20th Infy. Bn. (Cathal Brugha Barracks, Dublin)
21st Infy. Bn. (HQ & A Coy., Bray; B Coy. Dun Laoghaire; C Coy., Wicklow)
11th Cavalry Sqn. (Cathal Brugha Barracks, Dublin) - *equipped with four AML 245
H-60 armoured cars + soft-skinned vehicles.*
7th Field Arty. Rgt. (HQ, 14th Field & 19th Hvy. Mortar Btys. - McKee Barracks,
Dublin) - *equipped with twelve 120mm Brandt AM50 mortars*   2nd Air

Defence Bty. (Cathal Brugha Barracks, Dublin) - *equipped with six Bofors 40mm*
TABLE 15 (CONTINUED)

Mk 1 A/A guns (Subordinate to 1st Air Defence Rgt.)
11th Field Engineer Coy. (Clancy Barracks, Dublin)
11th Field Signals Coy. (Cathal Brugha Barracks, Dublin)
11th Field Supply & Transport Coy. (Collins Barracks, Dublin)
11th Field Medical Coy. (Cathal Brugha Barracks, Dublin)
6th Field Coy. Military Police (Collins Barracks, Dublin)

SOUTHERN COMMAND:

Command HQ (Collins Barracks, Cork)
3rd Maintenance Engineer Coy (Cork)
3rd Garrison Ordnance Coy. (Cork)
3rd Garrison Supply & Transport Cot (Cork)
3rd Hospital Coy. (Cork)
3rd Garrison Military Police Coy (Cork)
Command Training Depot (Cork)
Band of the Southern Command (Cork)

1st Infantry Brigade:

Bde. HQ (Collins Barracks, Cork)
4th Infy. Bn. (Cork)
12th Infy. Bn. (HQ, HQ Coy, A & C Coys., Limerick; B & Spt. Coy. Clonmel)
1st Cav. Sqn. (Fermoy) - *equipped with four AML 245 H-90 and six AML 245 H-60 armoured cars plus three AML VTT M3 APCs* 1st
Field Arty. Rgt. (HQ, 1st & 17th Field Btys. Balincollig) - *equipped with six 25 pounder gun-howitzers & six 120mm Brandt AM50m mortars*
1st Field Engineer Coy. (Cork)
1st Field Signals Coy. (Cork)
1st Field Supply & Transport Coy. (Cork)
1st Field Medical Coy. (FCA) (Cork)
1st Field Coy. Military Police (Cork)

Southern Command FCA Group:

TABLE 15 (CONTINUED)

HQ (Sarsefield Barracks, Limerick) 11th Infy. Bn. (HQ & A Coy., Bandon; B Coy., Bantry; C Coy., Clonakilty; D Coy Macroom; E Coy Skibbereen) 13th Infy. Bn. (HQ & A Coy., Fermoy; B Coy., Cahir; C Coy., Dungarvan; D Coy., Kanturk; E Coy., Mallow) 14th Infy. Bn. (HQ Limerick; A Coy., Nenagh; B Coy., Croom; C Coy., Kilmallock; D Coy., Newcastle West; E Coy., Tipperary)

15th Infy. Bn. (HQ & A Coy., Tralee; B Coy., Cahirciveen; C Coy., Dingle; E Coy., Killarney; E Coy., Killorglin; F Coy., Listowel) 22nd Infy. Bn. (HQ & A Coy., Ennis; B Coy., Lahinch; C Coy., Killaloe; D Coy., Kilrush) 23rd Infy. Bn. (HQ, A & B Coys. Cork; C Coy Middleton) 3rd Cav. Sqn. (Clonmel) - *equipped with four AML 245 H-60 armoured cars + soft-skinned vehicles* 8th Field Arty. Rgt. (HQ, 2nd Field & 21st Hvy. Mortar Btys. - Ballincollig) - *equipped with six 25 pounder gun-howitzers and six 120mm Brandt AM50 mortars* 3rd Air Defence Btys. (Limerick) - *equipped with six Bofors 40mm Mk 1 A/A guns.* (Subordinate to 1st Air Defence Rgt.) 4th Air Defence Bty. (Cobh) - *equipped with six Bofors 40mm Mk 1 A/A guns.* (Subordinate to 1st Air Defence Rgt.) 3rd Field Engineer Coy. (Limerick)

3rd Field Signals Coy. (Limerick)

3rd Field Supply & Transport Coy. (Limerick)

3rd Field Medical Coy. (Limerick)

3rd Field Coy. Military Police (Limerick)

WESTERN COMMAND

Command HQ (Custume Barracks, Athlone)
4th Maintenance Engineer Coy. (Athlone)
4th Garrison Ordnance Coy. (Athlone)
4th Garrison Supply & Transport Coy. (Athlone)
4th Hospital Coy (Athlone)
4th Garrison Coy. Military Police (Athlone)

TABLE 15 (CONTINUED)

Command Training Depot (Athlone)
University Student Admin. Coy. (Galway)
Band of the Western Command (Athlone)

4th Infantry Brigade:

Bde. HQ (Custume Barracks, Athlone)
1st Infy. Bn. (Galway)
6th Infy. Bn. (Athlone)
28th Infy. Bn. (HQ, HQ & C Coys., Finner Camp; A Coy., Lifford; B Coy.,
Letterkenny)
4th Cav. Sqn. (Longford) - *equipped with four AML 245 H-90 and six AML 245 H-60 armoured cars plus three AML VTT M3 APCs*

4th Field Arty. Rgt. (HQ, 8th Hvy. Mortar & 22nd Field Btys. - Mullingar) -
equipped with six 105mm Light Guns and six 120mm Brandt AM50 mortars
4th Field Engineer Coy. (Athlone)
4th Field Signals Coy. (Athlone)
4th Field Supply & Transport Coy. (Athlone)
4th Field Medical Coy. (FCA) (Athlone)

4th field Coy. Military Police (FCA) (Athlone)

Western Command FCA Group:

HQ (D' n Uì MhaoilÌosa, Galway)
16th Infy. Bn. (HQ & A Coy., Athlone; B Coy., Ballinasloe; C Coy., Tulamore; D
Coy. Roscommon)   17th
Infy. Bn. (HQ & A Coy., Longford; B Coy.,Granard; C Coy., Strokestown; D Coy.,
Ballyconnel; E Coy., Mohill)
18th Infy. Bn. (HQ & A Coy., Westport; B Coy., Enniscrone; C Coy., Swinford; D
Coy. Ballina)   19th
Infy. Bn. (HQ & A Coy., Boyle; B Coy., Carrick-on-Shannon; C Coy., Ballymote; D
Coy., Manorhamilton; E Coy., Castlerea)
24th Infy. Bn. (HQ & A Coy., Letterkenny; B Coy., Donegal; C Coy., Carndonagh; D
Coy., Milford)   25th Infy.
TABLE 15 (CONTINUED)

Bn. (HQ & A Coy., Galway; B Coy., Clifden; C Coy., Athenry; D Coy., Loughrea)

5th Cav. Sqn. (Castlebar) - *equipped with four AML 245 H-60 armoured cars + soft-skinned vehicles.*

5th Field Arty. Rgt. (HQ, 4th & 7th Field and 13th Heavy Mortar Btys. - Galway) ñ *equipped with six 25 pounder gun-howitzers and twelve 120mm Brandt AM50 mortars.*

9th Field Arty. Rgt. (HQ, 15th and 20th Field Btys., Mullingar) - *equipped with twelve 120mm Brandt AM50 mortars*

5th Field Engineer Coy (Galway).

5th Field Signals Coy. (Sligo)

5th Field Supply & Transport Coy (Galway)

5th Field Medical Coy (Galway)

5th Field Coy. Military Police (Galway)

CURRAGH COMMAND

HQ (Ceannt Barracks, Curragh Camp)

Military College (incorporating Infantry and Command & Staff Schools) (Curragh)

General Training Depot (Curragh)

No.1 Security Coy. (Portlaoise Prison)

Army Apprentice School (Naas)

Army Ranger Wing (Curragh) ñ *formed in 1980*

1st Tank Squadron (Plunkett Barracks, Curragh) ñ reactivated 1980 and equipped with fourteen Scorpion light tanks and five Timoney Mk VI APCs

Depot & School Cavalry (Curragh)

1st Anti-Aircraft Regiment (HQ & 1st Air Defence Bty., Kildare) - equipped with six 40mm Mk 1 Bofors A/A guns and six RBS 70 SAM launchers

Depot & School Artillery (Kildare)

1st Maintenance Engineer Coy (Curragh)

Depot & School Engineer Corps (Curragh)

Depot & School Signals Corps. (Curragh)

Curragh Command Supply & Transport Coy. (Curragh)

Curragh Command Vehicle Workshops (Curragh)

Depot & School Supply & Transport Corps (Curragh)

1st Garrison Ordnance Coy. (Curragh)

1st Hospital Coy. (Curragh)

General Military Hospital (Curragh)

Depot & School Medical Corps (Curragh)

Military Detention Barracks (Curragh)

TABLE 15 (CONTINUED)

Depot & School Military Police (Curragh)
Band of the Curragh Command (Curragh)

6th Infantry Brigade:

Bde. HQ (Connolly Barracks, Curragh)
3rd Infy. Bn. ì THE BLOODSî (Curragh) - *had one APC Coy. with twelve AML VTT M3 APCs*
30th Infy. Bn. (Kilkenny)
1st Armoured Sqn. (Plunkett Barracks, Curragh) - *equipped with three AML 245 H-90 and six AML 245 H60 armoured cars plus three AML VTT M3 APCs*
3rd Field Bty. (Curragh) - *equipped with six 105mm Light Guns (from 1981)*
6th Field Signal Coy. (Ceannt Barracks, Curragh)

Curragh Command FCA Group:

HQ (HQ Stephenís Barracks, Kilkenny)
9th Infy. Bn. (HQ & A Coy., Kilkenny; B Coy., Dunamaggin; C Coy., Ballyragget; D Coy., Waterford; E Coy., Portlaoise; F Coy. Durrow) *formed part of 6th Brigade from 1959-78*   10th Infy Bn.
ì OíHANRAHANî (HQ & A Coy., Wexford; B Coy., New Ross; C Coy., C Coy., Carnew; D Coy., Muinebeag; E Coy., Carlow) *formed part of 6th Brigade from 1959-78*   6th Field
Arty. Rgt. (HQ & 5th Field Bty., Kildare; 6th Field Bty., Naas; 11th Hvy. Mortar Bty., Edenderry) - *equipped with twelve 25 pounder gun-howitzers and six 120mm Brandt AM50 mortars*

Coast Artillery now finally disappeared from the order of battle. Spike Island, in Cork Harbour, became first a barracks for naval recruits and then a prison for young offenders. Fort Dunree, on Lough Swilly, was converted into a museum and the remaining installations were sold off and their equipment scrapped.

It will be noted that ì disintegrationî of the FCA from the PDF was not all embracing, the 1st Air Defence Regiment remaining fully integrated with a single regular and three FCA batteries. The Field Medical and Field Military Police Companies of the four surviving brigades also now became all FCA units. By way of consolation for its apparent downgrading in the over-all defence structure, the FCA had also acquired a new infantry battalion (25th in Galway), three new Artillery Regiments (7th in Dublin, 8th in Balincollig and 9th in Mullingar) to accommodate the six field batteries formerly integrated in the 1st, 2nd and 4th Artillery Regiments and a third Anti-Aircraft Battery (4th in Cobh). However, as nobody seemed to have any idea what to do with such a proliferation of independent units. they now formed an amorphous ì FCA Groupî in each of the four Commands.

There were other more significant developments afoot. The Minister for Defence had promised the introduction of women to the Defence Forces during a speech at a political party conference in 1978 and accordingly the first eight female cadets joined the Defence Forces on March 10th 1980. 40 female recruits followed these in June 1981 and women slowly became integrated into all branches of the Defence Forces, including the combat arms.

Six days after its first female cadets had been sworn in, on March 16th, 1980, the Irish Armyís first special forces unit, designated, the Army Ranger Wing, was officially established. Individual members of the Defence Forces had in fact completed Ranger courses abroad with the United States Army, the German Border Police and (although it has never been admitted) the British SAS, since the late 1960s but these had never been brought together in a permanent unit. The Irish Armyís Rangers, who are still enveloped in a cloak of romantic secrecy, approximate to an infantry rifle company in strength although their unit organization is radically different and they receive very comprehensive training in covert operations, hostage rescue, parachuting, diving, sniping etc. They also tend to favour different weapons to those in use by the remainder of the Defence Forces including ñ amongst the more orthodox - the Heckler & Koch HK 33 assault rifle, the HK 53 sub-machine gun and the FN Minimi light machine-gun.

The over all equipment situation of the Army had been steadily improving with the introduction of training quantities of the Euromissile Milan ATGW during the late 1970s and of the Bofors RBS-70 surface-to-air missile system, followed by the Ericsson Giraffe target acquisition and fire control system, in 1981. UN service had also underlined the lack of a heavy machine-gun and accordingly the veteran Browning M2 HB ì50 calibreî 12.7 mm was acquired and became standard equipment in 1984, initially at battalion and later at company level. New 60 and 81 mm mortars (the Hotchkiss-Brandt MO-60-63 60mm, MO-81-61L 81mm and MO-81-61C 81mm) also replaced existing equipment and finally the Steyer AUG ìUniversal Weaponî replaced both the FN FAL rifle and the Carl Gustav Kpist 45 sub-machinegun in service with the PDF. A Kevlar ballistic helmet of Israeli pattern was also adopted in the early 1980s.

In theory, each infantry battalion had one APC mounted and one truck-mounted company. Although equipment holdings and commitments to UN service meant that only three of the existing 11 Regular battalions had a full APC Company, by the mid 1980s each Infantry Battalion had a basic heavy equipment allocation of three APCs, four 90mm RCLs, seven 84mm rocket projectors, four 81mm mortars, six 60mm mortars, four 12.7mm and 27 7.62mm machine-guns. However, only Regular units had their full complement of support weapons and not al of these had even their minimal allocation of APCs.

The Army had been without even a token tank force since 1973. The acquisition of four Scorpion light tanks in 1980, followed by another four the following year and a third batch of four in 1982 permitted the revival of the 1st Tank Squadron but although two more vehicles were acquired in 1985, the armoured command, rescue and ambulance vehicles and the Stormer tracked APCs necessary to complete the organization of the squadron as a fully effective unit never materialized and as a stop-gap it was allocated first three Timoney Mk IV APCs and on the withdrawal of this type from service, five Timoney Mk VIs.

Following the first ìpre-productionî batch of Timoney Mk IV APCs, a second batch of five examples of the greatly improved Mk VI vehicle had been delivered in 1983 but although this vehicle was subsequently produced in quantity, under licence, in Belgium as the ìBDXî and another licence-built version was offered on the market by Vickers of Great Britain as the ìValkyrî, the Timoney vehicles were never ordered in quantity by the Irish Army.

With the acquisition of the full complement of the Panhard APCs, the Unimog scout cars were passed on to the FCA in 1978, the 3rd, 5th and 11th Squadrons receiving five vehicles apiece. Incredibly, the Landsverk and Leyland armoured cars, which had been handed over to the FCA Motor Squadrons in 1972, remained in service into the early 1980s, the 11th having five Landsverks while the 3rd and 5th had three Landsverks and three Leylands respectively. All the Motor Squadrons were re-designated ìCavalry Squadronsî in 1982.

The choice of a replacement for the British 25 pounder gun-howitzer as the main equipment of the field artillery had been the subject of consideration for many years although the security situation from 1969 had relegated this requirement to a secondary position. An original preference for the Oto Melara 105 mm pack howitzer was replaced by one for the British L-118 105 mm Light Gun that had entered service with the British Army during the interim and the first six-gun battery of this weapon was delivered in 1980. Sufficient material of this type to equip three more batteries was acquired at leisurely rate over the next 15 years.

Although the Lebanon operation was ongoing, the Irish Government had acceded in 1992 to a UN request for a military contribution to UNOSOM, the peacekeeping operation recently set up in Somalia which was racked by civil war and famine. Accordingly the 1st Transport Company was formed for UN service. The situation in Somalia had however already deteriorated so far that peacekeeping had escalated to peace-enforcement. As this was not covered by existing Irish legislation special legislation had to be enacted to permit this change in the mandate of Irish military forces on UN service and it was not until September 1993 that the 92 strong 1st Transport Company and its 34 vehicles departed for Somalia. After the usual six-month tour of duty this unit was relieved by the similarly constituted 2nd Transport Company, which served until the end of September 1994.

The disappearance of the Soviet Union and of the various puppet Communist regimes in Eastern Europe in 1989-90 resulted in a radical change in the global strategic picture which impacted not only on the defence policies of the major military powers but also on those of the neutral and non-aligned states of Europe. Accordingly, in the early 1990s the Irish Government commissioned international management consultants Price Waterhouse to carry out an Efficiency Audit of the Defence Forces.

This group published the first part of its Report, which dealt with the Army in detail, in 1994.

Amongst many recommendations for dealing with what was regarded as the excessive age profile of the Defence Forces in general and the excessive number of physically unfit members, the Report recommended the elimination of the four existing territorial commands; the establishment of a National Training Centre and Logistics Base for the Army; and a greater degree of autonomy for the Naval Service and Air Corps which should each resume responsibility for the many support functions, including engineering construction and maintenance, communications, general logistic, medical and military police services, for which it had hitherto depended on the Army. It also recommended the disposal of a number of what was regarded as the excessive number of military installations (29 barracks and 48 posts) and the civilianization of many services currently carried out by military personnel such as barracks catering and security. It also suggested a reduction in the existing number of military hospitals and army bands, queried the function of the Army Equitation School and specifically recommended the abolition of the Ordnance Survey Company of the Engineer Corps and the Army Catering School.

As regards tactical organization, the Efficiency Audit Group had examined three options for a one, two and three-brigade structure for the Army and concluded that the optimum would be a two-brigade force ñ one brigade with responsibility for the Border area and the other to cover the remainder of the country, except the Greater Dublin area which would be garrisoned by an independent battalion group with first call on the combat elements of the proposed National Training Centre (one Ranger company, one Light Tank squadron and an Air Defence Regiment).

Over all, the Report recommended the reduction in the peacetime establishment of the Army from its existing level of 12,623 to approximately 10,000.

Regarding the Reserves, the Report recommended the formalization of the existing de facto situation whereby some elements were still integrated with elements of the PDF by the formation of a two-tier Reserve, with differing degrees of liability for service and correspondingly of training. In effect, it recommended the abolition of the First Line Reserve, which had consisted of time expired members of the PDF who retained a liability for some reserve service and its replacement by a tier of the Army Reserve specifically designated to supply the shortfall in personnel between the peacetime and full wartime establishment of the PDF units. It further recommended that members of the Reserve who for one reason or another could not make the commitment to the degree of training required by the first tier but were still willing to serve in an emergency and undergo a lesser degree of training, should form a second tier which would man purely reserve units on mobilization.

Despite continued sporadic acts of terrorism by both Republican and ìLoyalistî splinter groups, the declaration in 1994 of a cease-fire by the IRA, the principal group of Republican terrorists active in Northern Ireland since 1969, followed four years later by the 1998 ìGood Friday Agreementî between the British and Irish Governments, which provided, inter alia, for a ìPower-Sharing Executiveî in Northern Ireland, considerably defused the security situation which had been the main pre-occupation of Irish defence and security planning and policy for the previous 25 years.

Although subsequently modified in detail, in the context of the improved security situation, the Government substantially accepted the recommendations of the Efficiency Audit Group and a three-year Implementation Plan was initiated in 1996.

The last Unimog armoured scout cars had finally been withdrawn in 1984, after six years service with FCA cavalry units. The Timoney Mk IV APCs followed these in 1988 although the Mk VIs soldiered on until 1999. Some measures were also taken to update the fleet of Panhard armoured cars and personnel carriers, which were beginning to show their age. All the armoured cars and 14 of the VTT APCs were re-engined with diesels during 1988-89, the H-90 armoured cars also receiving new gear-boxes in addition to laser range-finders and new fire direction and control systems for their 90 mm guns. The use of the mortars of the first batch of 16 H-60-7s had been prohibited following a series of mortar accidents in the late 1970s. As an interim measure, these now had both their twin 7.62 mm machine-guns and the useless 60 mm mortars replaced by a single 12.7 mm machine-gun in 1989. During the late 1990s the turrets of 16 of these vehicles were shipped to South Africa where they were fitted with 20 mm guns and fire direction and control systems in place of the 12.7 mm machine-guns. As modified, these vehicles were re-designated AML 245 H-20s. Strangely, 14 of the latter batch of 16 H-60-7HBs remained unmodified and they were placed on the disposal list, two being retained for upgrading to H-20 standards. The 14 VTT APCs re-engined with diesels were distributed between the 27th and 28th Border Battalions. Sixteen of the remainder were allocated to the 3rd Infantry Battalion, which remained the Armyís demonstration battalion, pending the acquisition of new APCs and the remainder were scrapped.

Two Finnish 6 x 6 SISU APCs had been acquired for training purposes in 1990, as these were now the most usual equipment of the Irish UN service units. The SISU was not chosen as the Irish Armyís new APC however and after evaluation of several types, including the 6 x 6 Austrian Steyer-Daimler-Puch PANDUR, an initial order was placed for 40 Mowag Piranha Mk IIIH 8 x 8 APCs as the first phase of re-equipment with this type of which it was intended to acquire at least 80. In the best traditions of Irish governmental parsimony in matters of defence, this order was subsequently modified to 34 examples of the basic APC, plus four command variants, one fittersí vehicle and one armoured ambulance. These were delivered during the latter part of 2001 and the first months of 2002. In the light of increasing UN commitments a further 25 units of the basic APC were subsequently ordered and these were in the process of delivery at the time of writing.

Although a range of new mortars had been introduced in the early 1980s, a new 60 mm weapon, the South African Vektor, began to enter service in the late 1990s. Other new equipment in the pipeline included the Bofors AT-4 84 mm disposable anti-armour weapon which was designated Short Range Anti-Armour Weapon (SRAAW) to avoid confusion with the 84 mm Carl Gustav RCL which remained in service although the more recent Pv-1110 90 mm RCL was withdrawn in the late 1990s. As a potential replacement for the latter weapon and the Euromissile Milan, 24 examples the Bofors Javelin ATGW were also placed on order.

Chapter 7 Leaner but Meaner (2000 to date)

The Irish Government published its first White Paper on Defence in February 2000. This formally enunciated its policy on defence for the first decade of the new millennium.

Despite the recommendations of the Efficiency Audit Group, an organization based on three regular Brigades was retained, as were the Equitation and Catering Schools. One of the four Army Bands was however suppressed as were two military hospitals (in the Southern and Western Command areas), the 1st Military Police Company and the Ordnance Survey Company of the Corps of Engineers and all training and logistic support elements not intrinsic to the Brigades were now concentrated at the Curragh. With a characteristic eye for penny-pinching, despite the Efficiency Groupís recommendation of an Army manpower establishment of 10,000, the White Paper set the establishment of the Permanent Defence Forces (including the Naval Service and Air Corps with combined establishments of over 2000) at 10,500 which indicated a total Army establishment of less than 8,500. The recommendations regarding the Reserves were accepted in toto but were not immediately implemented.

A number of the existing barracks and posts, which the Audit Group report had considered excessive, now also lost their permanent military presence and were gradually disposed of. These included Collins Barracks, Dublin, the worldís oldest continuously occupied military establishment; Griffiths and Clancy Barracks, also in Dublin; Magee Barracks, Kildare, the HQ of the Artillery since the late 1920s; Naas Military Barracks; Camp FitzGerald, Fermoy; and Murphy Barracks, Ballincollig.

By the end of 2000 the Chief of Staff was able to report the completion of the Implementation Plan as regards the re-organization of the PDF which now consisted of a slimmed down Headquarters numbering 293; Special Establishments (The Defence Forces School of Music with three Army Bands, the Army Equitation School, 1st Security Company at Port Laoise prison, McKee Barracks and Gormanston Camp Companies and camp staffs at Kilbride, Kilworth and Coolmoney Camps, plus the staff of the University Studentsí Administration and Service Company in Galway) with a total manpower of 407; 1,499 personnel in the combined National Training Centre and Logistics Base; plus three Brigades of 2330 each. The permanent staff of the Reserve Forces accounted for an additional 298, which together with 1,089 in the Navy and 924 in the Air Corps made a total Defence Forces strength of 11,500 or still 1,000 more than the target strength of 10,500.

The composition of the Army at the beginning of the new Millennium was as follows:

TABLE 16 ñ ORBAT 2000 ñ 2004

Army HQ:

Army HQ (Parkgate, Dublin)
Army HQ Signals Coy. (McKee Barracks, Dublin)
Army School of Music (Cathal Brugha Barracks, Dublin)
Army Equitation School (McKee Barracks, Dublin)
2nd Hospital Coy. (St. Bricinís Hospital, Dublin)
St. Bricinís Hospital (Dublin)
No. 1 Army Band (Cathal Brugha Barracks, Dublin)

2nd Eastern Brigade:

Bde. HQ (Collins Barracks, Dublin)
2nd Infy. Bn. (Cathal Brugha Barracks, Dublin)
5th Infy. Bn. (McKee Barracks, Dublin) - *equipped with seven AML VTT APCs*
27th Infy. Bn. (HQ, HQ Coy & A Coy., Dundalk; B Coy. Gormanston; Spt. Coy. Castleblaney)
2nd Cav. Sqn. (Cathal Brugha Barracks, Dublin) - *equipped with four AML 245 H-90 and four AML 245 H-20 armoured cars and soft-skinned vehicles*   2nd Field Arty. Rgt. (HQ, 10th & 18th Field Batteries - McKee Barracks, Dublin) - *equipped with six 105 mm light guns and six 25 pounder gun-howitzers*
2nd Field Engineer Coy. (McKee Barracks, Dublin)
2nd Field Signals Coy. (Cathal Brugha Barracks, Dublin)
2nd Logistic Bn. (Cathal Brugha Barracks, Dublin):

> 2nd Supply/Ordnance Company
> 2nd Field Transport Coy.
> 2nd Field Med. Coy

2nd Field Coy Military Police (Cathal Brugha Barracks, Dublin)
2nd Brigade Training Centre (Cathal Brugha Barracks, Dublin)

2nd Brigade FCA Group:

HQ (Cathal Brugha Barracks, Dublin)
7th Infy. Bn. (HQ & A & C Coys., McKee Barracks, Dublin; B Coy. Swords; D Coy., Navan; E Coy., Kells)
8th Infy. Bn. (HQ & A Coy., Dundalk; B Coy. Drogheda; C Coy., Castleblaney; D Coy. Cavan; E Coy., Balieboro)
20th Infy. Bn. (Cathal Brugha Barracks, Dublin)

T<small>ABLE</small> 16 (<small>CONTINUED</small>)

21st Infy. Bn. (HQ & A Coy., Bray; B Coy. Dun Laoghaire; C Coy., Wicklow)

11th Cavalry Sqn. (Cathal Brugha Barracks, Dublin) - *equipped with two AML 245 H-90 and two H-20 armoured cars + soft-skinned vehicles.*
7th Field Arty. Rgt. (HQ, 14th Field & 19th Hvy. Mortar Btys. - McKee Barracks, Dublin) *equipped with twelve 120mm Brandt AM50 mortars*
2nd Air Defence Bty. (Cathal Brugha Barracks, Dublin) - *equipped with six Bofors 40mm L/60 A/A guns* (Subordinate to 1st Air Defence Rgt.)
11th Field Engineer Coy. (McKee Barracks, Dublin)
11th Field Signals Coy. (Cathal Brugha Barracks, Dublin)
11th Field Transport Coy. (Cathal Brugha, Dublin)
11th Field Medical Coy. (Cathal Brugha Barracks, Dublin)
6th Field Coy. Military Police (Cathal Brugha Barracks, Dublin)

1st Southern Brigade:

Bde. HQ (Collins Barracks, Cork)
3rd Infantry Battalion (HQ, HQ Coy., A and Support Coys., Kilkenny; B Coy, Curragh) ëBí Coy *had one APC Coy. with sixteen AML VTT M3 APCs ñ replaced by Piranha Mk IIIs in 2001/2002*
4th Infy. Bn. (Cork)
12th Infy. Bn. (HQ, HQ Coy, A & C Coys., Limerick; B & Spt. Coy. Clonmel) 1st Cav. Sqn. (Cork) *equipped with four AML 245 H-90 and four AML 245 H-20 armoured cars and soft-skinned vehicles*
1st Field Arty. Rgt. (HQ, 1st & 17th Field Btys. Collins. Bks. Cork) *equipped with six 105 mm Light Guns & six 120mm Brandt AM50m mortars*   1st Field Engineer Coy. (Cork)
1st Field Signals Coy. (Cork)
1st Logistic Battalion (Cork):

1st Supply/Ordnance Coy.
1st Field Transport Coy.
1st Field Medical Coy.
1st Field Coy. Military Police (Cork)

Band of the 1st Brigade (Cork)

1st Brigade Training Centre (Cork)

TABLE 16 (CONTINUED)

1st Brigade FCA Group:

HQ (Sarsefield Barracks, Limerick)
11th Infy. Bn. (HQ & A Coy., Bandon; B Coy., Bantry; C Coy., Clonakilty; D Coy Macroom; E Coy Skibbereen)
13th Infy. Bn. (HQ & A Coy., Fermoy; B Coy., Cahir; C Coy., Dungarvan; D Coy., Kanturk; E Coy., Mallow)
14th Infy. Bn. (HQ Limerick; A Coy., Nenagh; B Coy., Croom; C Coy., Kilmallock; D Coy., Newcastle West; E Coy., Tipperary)
15th Infy. Bn. (HQ & A Coy., Tralee; B Coy., Cahirciveen; C Coy., Dingle; E Coy., Killarney; E Coy., Killorglin; F Coy., Listowel)
22nd Infy. Bn. (HQ & A Coy., Ennis; B Coy., Lahinch; C Coy., Killaloe; D Coy., Kilrush)
23rd Infy. Bn. (HQ, A & B Coys. Cork; C Coy Middleton)
3rd Cav. Sqn. (Clonmel) - *equipped two AML 245 H-90 and two H-20 armoured cars plus soft-skinned vehicles*
3rd Field Artillery Rgt. (HQ & 9th Field Bty. Templemore; 12th Field Bty. Birr; 16th Hvy. Mortar Bty. Thurles) - *equipped with six 25 pounder gun-howitzers and twelve 120mm Brandt AM50 mortars*
8th Field Arty. Rgt. (HQ, 2nd Field & 21st Hvy. Mortar Btys. ñ Collins Bks. Cork) - *equipped with six 25 pounder gun-howitzers and six 120mm Brandt AM50 mortars*
3rd Air Defence Bty. (Limerick) - *equipped with six Bofors 40mm L/60 A/A guns* (Subordinate to 1st Air Defence Rgt.)
4th Air Defence Bty. (Cobh) - *equipped with six Bofors 40mm L/60 A/A guns* (Subordinate to 1st Air Defence Rgt.)
3rd Field Engineer Coy. (Limerick)
3rd Field Signals Coy. (Limerick)
3rd Field Transport Coy. (Limerick)
3rd Field Medical Coy. (Limerick)

3rd Field Coy. Military Police (Limerick)

4th Western Brigade

Bde. HQ (Custume Barracks, Athlone)
1st Infy. Bn. (Galway)
6th Infy. Bn. (Athlone)

TABLE 16 (CONTINUED)

28th Infy. Bn. (HQ, HQ & C Coys., Finner Camp; A Coy., Lifford; B Coy., Letterkenny) - *equipped with seven AML VTT APCs*
4th Cav. Sqn. (Longford) - *equipped with four AML 245 H-90 and four AML 245 H-20 armoured cars and soft-skinned vehicles*
4th Field Arty. Rgt. (HQ, 8th Hvy. Mortar & 22nd Field Btys. - Mullingar) - *equipped with six 105mm Light Guns and six 120mm Brandt AM50 mortars*

4th Field Engineer Coy. (Athlone)
4th Field Signals Coy. (Athlone)
4th Logistic Battalion (Athlone):

> 4th Supply/Ordnance Coy.
> 4th Field Transport Coy.
> 4th Field Medical Coy.

4th field Coy. Military Police Coy. (Athlone)
Band of the 4th Brigade (Athlone)
4th Brigade Training Centre

4th Brigade FCA Group:

HQ (D' n Uì Mhaoilìosa, Galway)
16th Infy. Bn. (HQ & A Coy., Athlone; B Coy., Ballinasloe; C Coy., Tulamore; D Coy. Roscommon)
17th Infy. Bn. (HQ & A Coy., Longford; B Coy.,Granard; C Coy., Strokestown; D Coy., Ballyconnel; E Coy., Mohill)
18th Infy. Bn. (HQ & A Coy., Westport; B Coy., Enniscrone; C Coy., Swinford; D Coy. Ballina)
19th Infy. Bn. (HQ & A Coy., Boyle; B Coy., Carrick-on-Shannon; C Coy., Ballymote; D Coy., Manorhamilton; E Coy., Castlerea)
24th Infy. Bn. (HQ & A Coy., Letterkenny; B Coy., Donegal; C Coy., Carndonagh; D Coy., Milford)
25th Infy. Bn. (HQ & A Coy., Galway; B Coy., Clifden; C Coy., Athenry; D Coy., Loughrea)
5th Cav. Sqn. (Castlebar) - *equipped with two AML 245 H-90 and two H-20 armoured cars + soft-skinned vehicles.*
5th Field Arty. Rgt. (HQ, 4th & 7th Field and 13th Heavy Mortar Btys. ñ

TABLE 16 (CONTINUED)

Galway) - *equipped with six 25 pounder gun-howitzers and twelve 120mm Brandt AM50 mortars.*
9th Field Arty. Rgt. (HQ, 15th and 20th Field Btys., Mullingar) - *equipped*

Table 16 (continued

with twelve 120mm Brandt AM50 mortars
5th Field Engineer Coy (Galway).
5th Field Signals Coy. (Sligo)
5th Field Supply & Transport Coy (Galway)
5th Field Medical Coy (Galway)
5th Field Coy. Military Police (Galway)

Defence Forces Training Centre & Logistic Base

HQ (Ceannt Barracks, Curragh Camp)
Army Ranger Wing (Curragh)
1st Armoured Sqn. (Plunkett Barracks, Curragh) - *equipped with fourteen Scorpion light tanks*
Military College *(incorporating the Cadet School and the Infantry, Command & Staff and UN Schools)*(Curragh)
Combat Support College *(incorporating the Cavalry and Artillery Schools, and the Schools of Military Engineering and Signals)*
Combat Services Support College *(incorporating the Supply, Transport, Ordnance, Medical and Military Police Schools, the School of Administration and the School of Field Catering)*
Administrative & Support Unit
1st Air Defence Regiment Cadre (HQ & 1st Air Defence Bty., Kildare) - *equipped with six 40mm Bofors L/60 A/A guns and six RBS 70 SAM launchers*
1st Maintenance Engineer Coy (Curragh)
1st General Transport Coy. (Curragh)
Curragh Command Vehicle Workshops (Curragh)
1st Hospital Coy. (Curragh)
General Military Hospital (Curragh)
Military Detention Barracks (Curragh)
DFTC Military Police Company (Curragh)

TABLE 16 (CONTINUED)

DFTC FCA Group:

HQ (HQ Stephenís Barracks, Kilkenny)
9th Infy. Bn. (HQ & A Coy., Kilkenny; B Coy., Dunamaggin; C Coy., Ballyragget; D Coy., Waterford; E Coy., Portlaoise; F Coy. Durrow)
10th Infy Bn. (HQ & A Coy., Wexford; B Coy., New Ross; C Coy., C Coy., Carnew; D Coy., Muinebeag; E Coy., Carlow)
6th Field Arty. Rgt. (HQ & 5th Field Bty., Kildare; 6th Field Bty., Naas; 11th Hvy. Mortar Bty., Edenderry) - *equipped with twelve 25 pounder gun-howitzers and six 120mm Brandt AM50 mortars*
6th Field Signal Coy. (Ceannt Barracks, Curragh)

The four territorial Commands had disappeared as had the appointments of Adjutant General and Quarter Master General, which had been replaced by two Deputy Chiefs of Staff (Operations and Support). The Deputy Chief of Staff (Operations) was also now General Officer Commanding the Army by virtue of which he had an Assistant Chief of Staff of Brigadier General rank. Gone were the Engineer Corps Ordnance Survey Company and the 1st Garrison Military Police Company, which had previously been responsibility for security at Government Buildings, in Dublin. Gone also was the Band of the Curragh Command. All logistic support functions, other than those intrinsic to the Brigades, together with the National Training Centre, had been concentrated at the Curragh. The latter combined the Military College with the Combat Support College and the Combat Service Support College plus an Administrative and Supply unit and a Military Police Company. Somewhat inconsistently, both the Equitation and Music schools remained in Dublin although the Ranger Wing, 1st Armoured Squadron (former 1st Tank Squadron, which had changed its title when the 1st Armoured Car Squadron was stood down in 2000) and the Air Defence Regiment Cadre remained at the Curragh.

With the abolition of the Garrison, Supply & Transport, Ordnance and Military Police Companies these had been re-deployed and combined with the Field Supply and Transport and Medical Companies to form a Logistic Battalion (made up of a Supply/Ordnance, a Transport and a Medical Company) in each Brigade whilst the former Command Training Depots became Brigade Training Centres. With the introduction of PDF Medical and Military Police Companies to the Brigades these elements changed from predominantly FCA to predominantly PDF elements. Supply functions were also transferred from the Supply & Transport to the Ordnance Corps, leaving the former S&T Corps as the Transport Corps, with responsibility solely for transport functions and the maintenance of all the Armyís soft-skinned vehicles.

Following the terrorist attacks on the United States in September 2001 it was expected that the Irish Government would take measures to augment its totally deficient air defence system in the context of the total lack of fighter aircraft or even aircraft with any capability to intercept hostile aircraft within Irish airspace. The measures taken were as usual, parsimonious and half-baked when, following the rejection of a GIFT(!) of advanced trainer aircraft, with moderate air-to-air combat capabilities, offered by the Czech Republic, 30 Bofors EL/70 40 mm A/A guns and eight Signaal Flycatcher radar target acquisition and fire control systems were acquired, second-hand, from the Netherlands and 24 of these were used to replace the completely obsolete 40 mmL/60 guns which formed the tube-artillery equipment of the four batteries of the Irish Armyís sole Air Defence Regiment.

Requests for Irish military contributions to UN peacekeeping and peace-enforcement missions continued and the 1st to 3rd Guard & Administration Units served with UNMEE in Eritrea between December 2001 and November 2002. As indicated, these were largely logistic support units, with a small infantry and military police element for self-protection.

The Irish Government agreed to contribute a battalion to UNMIL in Liberia in 2003 and the 90th Infantry Battalion, numbering 427 all ranks, departed for service in December of that year being followed by the 91st Battalion six months later. At the time of writing. The 92nd Infantry Battalion was in the process of replacing the 91st. The Irish UNIMIL battalions include an APC mounted Infantry Company with 12 Mowag Piranha Mk IIIs and a troop of six H-20 armoured cars in their Support Companies. The 90th Battalion was also complemented by the deployment of a 36-man element of the Army Ranger Wing. Previous Irish peacekeeping forces had usually moved into prepared quarters. In Liberia they were however faced with a virgin site and therefore the UNIMIL operation involved the greatest logistic effort of any Irish peace-keeping operation to date with equipment weighing 1,756 tonnes and including approximately 170 vehicles, together with 474 personnel, were moved in eight airlifts ñ three of personnel and five of cargo ñ and one sea-lift, over a period of 28 days. A month before the deployment of the 90th Battalion a total of 129 personnel, including a special operations task group, a 40 man Engineer Platoon, with 30 additional construction personnel, a security platoon and a communications detachment, spent four weeks in Liberia preparing base facilities.

Ireland had joined the NATO sponsored Partnership for Peace in 1999 and Irish military participation in international peace-keeping and enforcement activities entered a new dimension with the participation, commencing in September 1999, of the first of eight Transport Companies (numbered 1st to 8th) in KFOR, a UN mandated operation in Kosovo, carried out under the auspices of NATO. The 27th Infantry Group relieved the 8th Transport Company in October 2003 and this unit was in turn followed by the 28th Infantry Group, which served until October 2004. These Infantry Groups were a new type of unit numbering 261 in all and including a Logistic Support Company, numbering 55 and an

APC mounted Infantry Company, numbering 141 and instead of serving as an autonomous element combined with Finnish troops in a multi-national battalion.

Chapter 8 An Army for the New Millennium?

The FCA had continued to languish in a state of military limbo since the abandonment of the integrated organization in 1979 having even suffered the further indignity of having its annual full-time training period reduced from 14 to seven days, as an economy measure, during the early 1980s. The only gestures towards an operational role had been the establishment of a Directorate of Reserve Forces at Army HQ in 1979 and in 2002, for no obvious reason other than that it was the nearest permanently manned military base to the constituency of the then Minister for Defence, this entity had been re-located to Clonmel.

In July 2004 the long awaited Implementation Plan for the Review of the Reserve Forces was unveiled. Following the very broad lines laid down in the White Paper, this provided for a two-tier Reserve with the more highly trained tier providing a third rifle company for each of the nine Regular infantry battalions; a third field battery and an air-defence battery for each of the three artillery regiments; three additional batteries for the Air Defence Regiment and sufficient manpower to bring all elements of the PDF up to full establishment strength. The second tier, with a lower commitment to training and service, would provide three Reserve brigades, to shadow the three Regular brigades, relieve them of garrison functions and provide them with a pool of trained replacements. The first ì integratedî tier was to number 2,656 whilst the second ì non-integratedî tier had an establishment of 9,292 giving a total establishment for the new Army Reserve of 11,948.

The anomalous title of ì FCAî, with its territorial connotations, was also now officially changed to ì Army Reserveî.

The new Reserve Brigades were to be numbered 3rd (Southern), 5th (Western) and 6th (Eastern) and apart from the initial omission of the Supply/Ordnance Company from their Logistic Battalions would closely follow the structure of the PDF formations.

The organization of the new Army Reserve at unit level would however depart radically from that in existence, with minor changes, since 1959. The reduction of the existing number of infantry battalions from eighteen to nine would involve the merger of the 9th and 10th; the 11th;13th and 23rd; the 14th, 15th and 22nd; the 16th and 17th; the 18th and 25th; the 19th and 24th; and the 20th and 21st Battalions to become, respectively, the new 62nd, 65th, 67th, 32nd, 33rd, 34th, 51st, 56th and 58th Reserve Infantry Battalions. Likewise the reduction of the six existing artillery regiments involved the fusion of the 6th and 7th; the 3rd and 8th; and the 5th and 9th to become the new 62nd, 31st and 54th Reserve Artillery Regiments.

A well-hidden logic underlay the apparently random numbering of the new units. This reflected the pairing of Reserve with PDF units to form something closely resembling a regimental system. Thus the new 62nd, 65th and 67th Infantry Battalions, whilst obviously deriving the first digit of their numerical designation from that of their parent Brigade, derived the second digit from that of the Regular unit with which they were effectively paired, in this case the 2nd, 5th and 2(7)th Battalions of the 2nd Brigade. This system was to be repeated consistently throughout each unit of the three new Brigades, the proposed changes in the organization of which are shown graphically in the following Table:

TABLE 17 ñ ARMY RESERVE FORCE REORGANIZATION 2004

EXISTING RESERVE UNITS		NEW RESERVE UNITS
Eastern Command/2nd Brigade FCA Group	to become -	6th Eastern Reserve Brigade
20th & 21st Infy. Bns. FCA	to become -	62nd Reserve Infy. Bn
7th Infy. Bn. FCA	to become -	65th Reserve Infy. Bn.
8th Infy. Bn. FCA	to become -	67th Reserve Infy. Bn.
11th Cav. Sqn. FCA	to become -	62nd Reserve Cav. Sqn.
6th Field Arty. Rgt. FCA (DFTC)	to become -	62nd Reserve Arty. Rgt.
7th Field Arty. Rgt. FCA	to become -	62nd Reserve Arty. Rgt.
11th Field Engr. Coy FCA	to become -	62nd Reserve Engr. Coy.
11th Field Signals Coy.	to become -	62nd Reserve CIS Coy
2nd & 6th Field MP Coys. FCA	to become -	62nd Reserve MP Coy.
11th Field Tpt. Coy. FCA	to become -	62nd Reserve Logs. Bn.
11th & 27th Field Medical Coy.	to become -	62nd Reserve Logs. Bn.
DFTC FCA Group	To be suppressed	
9th & 10th Infy. Bns. FCA*	to become -	33rd Reserve Infy. Bn.
6th Field Arty. Rgt. FCA*	to become -	62nd Reserve Arty. Rgt.
Southern Command/1st Brigade FCA Group	to become -	3rd Southern Reserve Brigade
14th, 15th & 22nd Infy. Bns. FCA	to become -	32nd Reserve Infy. Bn.
9th & 10th Infy. Bns. FCA (DFTC)	to become -	33rd Reserve Infy. Bn.
11, 13th & 23rd Infy Bns. FCA	to become -	34th Reserve Infy. Bn.
3rd Cav. Sqn. FCA	to become -	31st Reserve Cav. Sqn.
3rd & 8th Field Arty. Rgts. FCA	to become -	31st Reserve Arty. Rgt.
3rd Field Engr. Coy FCA	to become -	31st Reserve Engr. Coy.
31st Signals Coy. FCA	to become -	31st Reserve CIS Company
1st & 3rd Field MP Coys.	to become -	31st Reserve MP Coy.
3rd Field Tpt. Coy.	to become -	31st Reserve Logs. Bn.
1st & 3rd Field Medical Coys. FCA	to become -	31st Logs. Bn.

TABLE 17 (CONTINUED)

EXISTING RESERVE UNITS		NEW RESERVE UNITS
Western Command /4th Brigade FCA Group	- to become -	5th Western Reserve Brigade
18th & 25 Infy. Bns. FCA	to become -	51st Reserve Infy. Bn.
16th & 17th Infy. Bns. FCA	to become -	56th Reserve Infy. Bn.
19th & 24th Infy. Bns. FCA	to become -	58th Reserve Infy. Bn.
5th Cav. Sqn. FCA	to become -	54th Reserve Cav. Sqn.
5th & 9th Field Arty. Rgts. FCA	to become -	54th Reserve Arty. Rgt.
5th Field Engineer Coy. FCA	to become -	54th Reserve Engr. Coy.
5th Signals Coy. FCA	to become -	54th Reserve CIS Coy.
4th & 5th Field MP Coys. FCA	to become -	54th Reserve MP Coy.
5th Field Tpt. Coy FCA	to become -	54th Reserve Logs. Bn.
5th Field Medical Coy. FCA	to become -	54th Reserve Logs. Bn.

The amalgamation of existing and the establishment of new units is scheduled to be completed in October 2005 when the Order of Battle of the combined PDF and Reserve should be as in Table 18.

TABLE 18 ñ PROJECTED ORBAT 2005 ONWARDS

Army HQ

Army HQ CIS Company (Dublin)
2nd Hospital Coy. (St. Bricinís Military Hospital, Dublin)
Army School of Music & No. 1 Army Band (Cathal Brugha Bks., Dublin)
Army Equitation School (McKee Barracks, Dublin)

1st (Southern) Brigade (HQ Cork):

HQ (Collins Bks., Cork)
3rd Infy. Bn. (HQ, HQ Coy, ì Aî Coy & Support Coy. Stephens Bks.,
Kilkenny; ì Bî Coy. Connolly Bks., Curragh)
4th Infy. Bn. (Collins Bks., Cork)
12th Infy. Bn. (HQ, HQ COY &î Aî Coy Sarsfield Bks., Limerick; ì Bî Coy &
Support Coy Kickham Bks., Clonmel)
1st Cavalry Sqn. (Collins Bks., Cork)
1st Artillery Rgt. (Collins Bks., Cork)
1st Engineer Coy. (Collins Bks., Cork)
1st CIS Coy. (Collins Bks., Cork)
1st Logistic Bn. (Collins Bks., Cork)
1st Military Police Company (Collins Bks., Cork)
1st Brigade Depot & Training Centre (Collins Bks., Cork)
Band of 1st Bde. (Collins Bks. Cork)

3rd (Southern) Reserve Brigade (HQ Limerick?)

HQ
32nd Reserve Infy. Bn. (Tralee)
33rd Reserve Infy. Bn. (Wexford)
34th Reserve Infy. Bn. (Fermoy)
31st Reserve Cav. Sqn. (Clonmel)
31st Reserve Arty. Rgt. (Templemore)
31st Reserve Engineer Coy. (Limerick)
31st Reserve CIS Coy. (Limerick)
31st Reserve Logistic Bn. (Limerick)
31st Reserve MP Coy. (Limerick)
3rd Brigade Depot & Training Centre (Limerick)

TABLE 18 (CONTINUED)

2nd (Eastern) Brigade (HQ Dublin):

    HQ (Cathal Brugha Bks., Dublin)
    2nd Infy Bn. (Cathal Brugha Bks., Dublin)
    5th Infy. Bn. (HQ, HQ Coy, ì Aî Coy & Support Coy McKee Bks. Dublin; ì Bî Coy. Gormanston Camp)
    27th Infy Bn. (HQ, HQ Coy, ì Aî Coy and Support Coy. Aiken Bks. Dundalk; ì Bî Coyî Monaghan)
    2nd Cavalry Sqn. (Cathal Brugha Bks., Dublin)
    2nd Artillery Rgt. (McKee Bks., Dublin)
    2nd Engineer Coy. (Cathal Brugha Bks., Dublin)
    2nd CIS Coy. (McKee Bks., Dublin)
    2nd Logistic Bn. (Cathal Brugha Bks., Dublin)
    2nd Military Police Company (Cathal Brugha Bks., Dublin)
    2nd Brigade Depot & Training Centre (Cathal Brugha Bks., Dublin)

6th (Eastern) Reserve Brigade (HQ Dublin)

    HQ (McKee Bks. Dublin)
    62nd Reserve Infy. Bn. (Cathal Brugha Bks. Dublin)
    63rd Reserve Infy. Bn. (McKee Bks. Dublin)
    67th Reserve Infy. Bn. (Dundalk)
    62nd Reserve Cav. Sqn. (Cathal Brugha Bks. Dublin)
    62nd Reserve Artillery Rgt. (McKee Bks. Dublin)
    62nd Reserve Engineer Coy. (McKee Bks. Dublin)
    62nd Reserve CIS Coy. (Cathal Brugha Bks. Dublin)
    62nd Reserve Log. Bn. (Cathal Brugha Bks. Dublin)
    6th Brigade Depot & Training Centre

4th (Western) Brigade (HQ Athlone):

    HQ (Custume Bks., Athlone)
    1st Infy Bn. (D˙ n UÌ Mhailìosa, Galway)
    6th Infantry Bn. (Custume Bks. Athlone & Monaghan)
    28th Infy. Bn. (Finner, Lifford & Letterkenny)
    4th Cavalry Sqn. (Connolly Bks., Longford)
    4th Artillery Rgt. (Columb Bks., Mullingar)
    4th Engineer Coy. (Custume Bks., Athlone)
    4th CIS Coy. (Custume Bks., Athlone)
    4th Logistic Bn. (Columb. Bks. Mullingar) 4th Military Police Company (Custume Bks., Athlone)
    4th Brigade Depot & Training Centre (Custume Bks., Athlone)
    Band of 4th Bde. (Custume Bks. Athlone)

TABLE 18 (CONTINUED)

5th (Western) Reserve Brigade (HQ Galway?)

> HQ (Galway?)
> 51st Reserve Infy. Bn. (Galway)
> 56th Reserve Infy. Bn. (Athlone)
> 58th Reserve Infy. Bn. (Finner Camp, Bundoran)
> 54th Reserve Cav. Sqn. (Longford)
> 54th Reserve Arty. Rgt. (Mullingar)
> 54th Reserve Engineer Coy. (Galway)
> 54th Reserve CIS Coy. (Athlone)
> 54th Logistic Bn. (Galway)
> 54th Reserve MP Coy. (Athlone)
> 5th Brigade Depot & Training Centre

Defence Forces Training Centre & Logistic Base (Curragh):

> HQ DFTC&LB
>
> Army Ranger Wing
> 1st Armoured Cavalry Squadron
> 1st Air Defence Regiment (cadre)

Defence Forces Training Centre:

> Military College
> Combat Support College:
> Combat Support Services College:
> Educational Resources Centre
> Administrative Support Unit
> DFTC Military Police Coy.

Defence Forces Logistic Base:

> Supply Depot1st Construction & Maintenance Engineer Company
> 1st General Transport Company
> Base Workshops
> 1st Technical Workshops Coy.
> 1st Hospital Coy. (Curragh Military Hospital)

That is the theory. Apart from the Herculean task of training and equipping the Reserves to a level adequate to permit them to carry out their greatly expanded task, this must be accomplished in the context of the requirement of further reductions in the PDF element of the Army and the Governmentís pledge to provide an 850 strong mechanized infantry battalion for the proposed EU Rapid Reaction Force in addition to an on-going commitment of at least one battalion to international peace-keeping and/or peace-enforcement operations.

At the end of 2003 the overall strength (but not the establishment) of the Permanent Defence Force was 10,497. This included 1,065 in the Naval Service (establishment 1,144) and 903 in the Air Corps (establishment 930) leaving a total of 8,529 men and women in the Army for which the establishment was still 8,706.

The peacetime establishment of each of the Armyís three Regular Brigades remains at 2,330 although the most recent figure for the actual strength of the 1st Southern Brigade was 2,007 (86% of establishment); that for the 2nd Eastern Brigade was 2,398 (102% of establishment!); and that for the 4th Western Brigade 2,277 (98% of establishment), whilst that of the National Training centre and Logistic Base was 1,576 or 122% of its establishment of 1,294 leaving, apparently, only 271 to be divided between Defence Forces HQ, Special Establishments and the PDF cadre of the Reserve Forces!

If the present establishments of the Naval Service and Air Corps (both of which appear minimal) are to be maintained, this leaves only 8,426 for the reduced establishment of the Army within the officially authorized envelope of 10,500. Deducting 6,990 for the three Regular Brigades, plus 1,294 for the Defence Forces Training Centre and Logistic Base (which also includes the Army Ranger Wing, the 1st Armoured Squadron and the cadre of the Air Defence Regiment!) this leaves only 142 to be divided between Defence Forces HQ, Special Establishments and the PDF cadre of the Reserve Forces.

The figures do not add up nor does there seem to be any scope for a reduction in the already very lean peacetime establishments of the three Regular Brigades, much less that of the Defence Forces Training Centre and Logistic Base. The politicians who have come up with the apparently arbitrary target figure of 10,500 for the combined Permanent Defence Forces have hived off this manifestly impossible task to their Chief of Staff. Bearing in mind the very respectable ì tooth to tailî ratio of approximately 80% combat arms to 20% headquarters and supporting services already achieved and that the Efficiency Audit Group estimated that a total establishment of 10,000 would be necessary for the Army alone, on the basis of a smaller force of two brigades and a battalion group, his job in this respect, is not an enviable one.

Postscript

The geographical position of Ireland, with two major military powers, the United States to the west and Britain to the east, insulates it from any serious military threat by a third country. For their own security, it also obliges both the US and the UK either to occupy or defend the Republic. Britain having disengaged from more than three centuries of military occupation of southern Ireland in 1921 has shown no inclination to repeat this exercise and indeed the only serious threat of invasion, which independent Ireland has suffered, was in 1943 when it defied a US ultimatum to expel Axis diplomats.

During the post World War II period Ireland refused to become a member of NATO, with which its national interests were certainly more closely identifiable than with those of the Warsaw Pact, membership of which was never even contemplated. This decision was rationalized on the grounds that the NATO Treaty obliged its members to respect their mutual existing boundaries. The continued occupation of the north eastern part of the country, which as we have seen, was somewhat ironically the main reason why Britain did not seek to re-occupy southern Ireland's sea ports and air bases during World War II, was given as the justification for this stance although countries such as Greece and Turkey, whose conflicting territorial claims and other differences dated back at least to the Trojan War, found no such problem.

Whilst making no adequate provisions for its own defence throughout the Cold War, thanks to its geographical situation, the Republic was able to indulge in a form of pseudo-neutrality under the NATO umbrella, which, with considerable justification, has been described as ìparasiticî. Even after the collapse of the Soviet Union and the end of Communism in Eastern Europe anything smacking of NATO retained pejorative connotations in Ireland which was one of the last countries to subscribe to the NATO sponsored Partnership for Peace.

Nevertheless, the Irish Defence Forces, although starved of resources, both human and material, have always maintained the highest standards of professionalism, as has been endorsed by repeated requests for their participation in international peace-keeping and more recently peace-enforcement operations. Within the straitjacket of a politically imposed manpower establishment which is unrealistically low relative to their organizational structure (especially in the case of the Army) they are now also better-equipped and more realistically organized than at any time in their relatively short history. The recent rationalization of the role and re-organization of the Reserves, provided that it does not suffer the fate of the 1959 ìIntegrationî, also seems to make the best possible use of this long-neglected asset.

Appendix I: Irish UN and Other Peace-Keeping Service Units

Unit	Mission	Period of Service
32nd to 39th Infantry Bns.	ONUC	July 1960 -May 1964
1st Infantry Grp.	ONUC	May -Nov. 1961
2nd Infantry Grp.	ONUC	Nov. 1963 - May 1964
2nd & 3rd Armd. Sqns	ONUC	Oct 1962 - Oct. 1963
40th to 42nd Infantry Bns.	UNFICYP	Apr. 1964 - Oct. 1965
3rd to 24^{th*} Infantry Grps.	UNFICYP	Aug. 1964 - May. 1974
24^{th*} to 26th Infantry Grps.	UNEF	Apr.- May 1974
43rd to 89th Infantry Bns.	UNIFIL	Apr. 1978 ñ Nov. 2001
27th & 28th Infantry Grps	UNIFIL	Apr. 1973 ñ April 1974
90th to 92nd Infantry Bns.	UNMIL	Oct. 2003 - Mar. 2005
1st to 3rd Guard & Admin Units	UNMEE	Dec. 2001 ñ Nov. 2002
1st & 2nd Transport Coys	UNOSOM	Sept. 1993 - Sept. 1994
1st to 8th Transport Coys.	KFOR	Sept. 1993 ñ Sept. 2003
27th & 28th Infantry Grps.	KFOR	Oct. 2003 ñ Oct. 2004

NOTE: The above list refers only to tactical units of company size or greater which have taken part in peacekeeping and peace-enforcement operations. In addition to these, numbers of Irish troops varying from two to almost 200 have taken part in UN operations in West New Guinea (UNTEA), in 1962; on the frontier between India and Pakistan (UNMOGIP & UNGOMAP), in 1987-92; the Golan Heights (UNDOF), 1974 to date; Iran and Iraq (UNIT & UNIIMOG), 1984-91; Afghanistan and Pakistan (UNGOMAP & OSGA), 1984 to date; Namibia (UNTAG), 1989-90; Central America (ONUCA & ONUSAL), 1989-94; Iraq-Kuwait (UNIKOM), 1991 to date; Angola (UNAVEM II), 1991-93; Western Sahara (MINURSO), 1991 to date; Cambodia (UNTAC), 1991-93; Yugoslavia (UNMLO-Y), 1992 to date; and Haiti (UNMIH), 1994 to date.

Appendix II: Organization of Typical Irish Army UN Service Battalion

<u>66th Battalion - UNIFIL 1989-90</u> (TOTAL STRENGTH: 681)

HQ Coy (217)

      HQ (11)
      Admin Pln. (33)
      Logistics Pln. (44)
      Tpt. Pln. (44)
      Med. Pln. (21)
      Engineer Pln. (27)
      Signals Pln. (37)

A Coy (127)

      HQ
      No. 1 Pln. - *2 x 7.6 mm MAGs*
      No. 2 Pln. - *2 x 7.6 mm MAGs*
      Support Weapons Pln. - *1 x 84 mm RCL; 2 x 12.7 mm MGs*

B Coy (127)

      HQ
      No. 3 Pln. - *2 x 7.6 mm MAGs*
      No. 4 Pln. - *2 x 7.6 mm MAGs*
      Support Weapons Pln. - *1 x 84 mm RCL; 2 x 12.7 mm MGs*

C Coy (127)

      HQ
      No. 5 Pln. - *2 x 7.6 mm MAGs*
      No. 6 Pln. - *2 x 7.6 mm MAGs*
      Support Weapons Pln. - *1 x 84 mm RCL; 2 x 12. 7 mm MGs*

Recce. Coy. (83)

      HQ (6)
      Recce. Pln. (25) - *4 x AML H-90 armd. Cars. + 10 SISU APCs*
      Mortar Pln. (28) - *4 x AM50 120 mm mortars; 4 x 81 mm mortars*
      A/T Pln. (15) - *4 x Pv-1110 90 mm RCLs*
      Tech. Secn. (9)

Appendix III: AFVs of the Irish Army

TANKS

  1 x Vickers Medium ì Dî *(acquired 1929)*
  2 x Vickers Carden-Loyd Tankettes *(order cancelled)*
  2 x Landsverk L-60 *(acquired 1935-36)*
  4 x Churchill *(acquired 1948-49)*
  8 x Comet *(acquired 1958-59)*
  14 Scorpion *(four acquired in 1980; four in 1981; four in 1982, two in 1985)*

Tracked Carriers

  226 x Universal Carriers *(26 acquired in 1940; 200 more in 1942)*

Armoured Cars

  13 x Rolls Royce *(acquired 1922)*
  7 x Peerless *(acquired 1922)*
  64 x Lancia *(acquired 1922)*
  4 x Leyland *(built on Leyland Terrier truck chassis 1935)*
  8 x Landsverk L-180 *(two in 1938; 6 in 1939; five more seized by Swedish
        Government 1942 and never delivered)*
  1 x Morris *(unsuccessful proto-type built 1940)*
  7 x Ford Mk IV *(built on Ford truck chassis 1940)*
  14 x Ford Mk V *(built on Ford truck chassis 1940)*
  21 x Ford Mk VI *(built on Ford truck chassis 1941)*
  2 x Dodge Mk VII *(built on Dodge truck chassis 1942)*
  3 x Dodge Mk VIII *(built on Dodge truck chassis 1943)*

  16 x AML 245 H-60-7 *(16 acquired, in two batches of eight each, in 1964)*
  16 x AML 245 H-60-7 HB *(16 acquired during 1973-74)*
  20 x AML 245 H-90 *(four acquired in 1972; 16 more during 1973-74)*
  16 x AML 245 H-13 *(rebuilt H-60-7s with Diesel engines and 0.50î MG in place
        of 60 mm gun-mortar)*
  18 x AML 245 H-20 *(rebuilt H-13s; Diesel engines; 20 mm gun replaced 0.50î
  MG)*
  10 x Mk III Beaverette Scout Cars *(acquired 1943)*
  20 x Mk IV Beaverette Scout Cars *(acquired 1943)*
  15 Landsverk-Unimog Armoured Scout Cars *(acquired 1972)*

<u>Wheeled Armoured Personnel Carriers</u>

60 x AML VTT M-3 *(17 in 1972; 23 more, including 4 command post variants, in 1973-74 and 20 in 1975)*
5 x Timoney Mk IV *(five acquired in 1977)*
5 x Timoney Mk VI *(five acquired in 1981)*
2 x Sisu XA-120 *(two acquired in 1990)*
65 x Mowag Piranha IIIH *(40 including 4 command post, 1 ambulance and 1 repair vehicle variants delivered 2002; 25 more delivered 2004-2005). At least 15 more to be acquired.*

Appendix IV: Artillery Equipment of the Irish Army

FIELD ARTILLERY

6 x 60 pdr guns *(two acquired 1942; four more in 1943)*
32 x 18 pdr guns *(5 Mk II, 4 Mk I in 1922; 1 in 1925; 3 in 1933-34; 11 in 1934-1939; 4 in 1941; 4 in 1942)*
4 x 4.5" howitzers *(4 in 1925; 14 in 1940; 4 in 1941; 20 in 1942-43)*
4 x 3.7" howitzers *(acquired during 1933-34)*
8 x 75 mm guns *(ex-US; acquired 1942)*
48 x 25 pdr Mk II gun-howitzers *(All acquired 1949)*
72 x Brandt M50A 120 mm mortars *(All acquired 1954)*
24 x RA 105 mm Light Guns *(Acquired from late 1970s to mid 1990s)*

Coast Artillery

6 x 9.2" *(Handed over by Britain 1938)*
10 x 6" *(Eight Handed over by Britain 1938; two more acquired 1942)*
2 x 4.7" *(Two acquired 1942)*
21 x 12 pdrs *(Handed over by Britain 1938)*

Anti-Tank Weapons

7 x 2 pdr *(one acquired 1940; six more in 1943)*
1 x 6 pdr *(From scrapped ì Medium Dî tank)*
6 x 6 pdr *(Acquired late 1940s)*
12 x 17pdr *(acquired 1950s)*
96 x Bofors PV-1110 90 mm RCL *(acquired during 1960s)*
21 x Milan ATGWs *(acquired from 1979 onwards)*
36 x Javelin ATGW *(in course of acquisition 2004)*

Anti-Aircraft Weapons

4 x 3" 20 cwt
19 x 3.7" (Two acquired 1940; 5 more in 1941; 8 in 1942; 4 in 1943)
24 x Bofors 40 mm/L60 (4 in 1940; 2 in1942-43; 18 more acquired after 1945)
2 x Bofors 40 mm/L70 (acquired late 1950s)
30 x Bofors 40 mm EL/70 (acquired 2002)
7 x RBS-70 SAM launchers acquired from 1981 onwards

Appendix V: Army Strength 1969/1977

ELEMENT	STRENGTH 1969	AS % OF TOTAL	STRENGTH 1977	AS % OF TOTAL
STAFF	516	8.58%	604	4.54%
INFANTRY	1476	24.53%	5781	43.41%
CAVALRY	319	5.30%	788	5.92%
ARTILLERY	474	7.88%	974	7.31%
ENGINEERS	421	6.99%	666	5.00%
SIGNALS	246	4.10%	604	4.54%
ORDNANCE	319	5.30%	505	3.79%
SUPPLY & TPT.	457	7.60%	791	5.94%
MEDICAL	284	4.72%	426	5.59%
MIL. POLICE	336	4.18%	556	5.94%
OBSERVER CORPS	19	0.32%	19	0.14%
OTHERS	1258	20.91%	1602	12.03%
COMBAT TROOPS	2690	44.72%	8209	61.65%
SUPPORT TROOPS	3325	55.28%	5107	38.35%
Total	6015	100.00%	13316	100.00%
% OF ESTABLISHMENT		84.79%		91.00%

The peacetime establishment (sanctioned) strength in 1969 was 11,710. In 1977 it was 15,783 (see Appendix VI below)

Appendix VI: Army Establishment 1977

Infantry: (6,528 all ranks): 29 Battalions (18 FCA), 2 barracks security coys., 1 prison security coy. and 1 Ranger Unit.
Cavalry: (842 all ranks): Depot, 1 Tank Squadron, 1 Armoured & 6 Mechanized Reconnaissance Squadrons (3 FCA)
Artillery: (1,290 all ranks): Depot, 9 Field Arty. Rgts. (6 FCA) & 1 Air Defence Rgt. (1 Regular & 3 FCA A/A Btys.)
Engineers: (744 all ranks): Depot, 6 Field Engineer Coys. (3 FCA), 5 Construction Coys. & 1 Survey Coy.
Signals: (818 all ranks): Depot, 1 Army HQ Signal Coy., 6 Field Signal Coys (3 FCA) & 1 Air Corps Signals Coy
Ordnance Corps: (759 all ranks): Depot + 4 Garrison Coys.
Supply & Transport Corps: (986 all ranks): Depot, 4 Garrison Coys. & 6 Field Coys (3 FCA)
Military Police (864 all ranks): Depot, 4 Garrison Coys. (All regular) & 6 Field Coys. (All FCA)
Medical Corps: (599 all ranks): Depot, 4 Hospital Coys. (All regular) & 6 Field Coys. (All FCA)
Miscellaneous: (2,353 all ranks)

TOTAL ESTABLISHMENT: 15,783 all ranks

The above figures obviously referred only to figures for the PDF and the permanent training cadres of the FCA and did not take into account the largely theoretical establishment of the latter element.

Appendix VII: Army Sanctioned Strength vs. Actual (1977)

Element	Sanctioned	% Of Sanctioned	Actual	% Of Total
Infantry	6528	41.36%	5781	88.56%
Cavalry	842	5.33%	788	93.56%
Artillery	1290	8.17%	974	75.50%
Engineers	744	4.71%	666	89.52%
Signals	818	5.18%	604	73.84%
S&T	759	4.81%	505	66.53%
Ordnance	986	6.25%	791	80.22%
Medical	599	3.80%	426	71.12%
Mil. Police	864	5.47%	556	64.35%
Others	2353	14.91%	2225	94.56%
Total	15783	100.00%	13316	84.37%

Appendix VIII: Irish Army Infantry Battalion 1978 ñ Peacetime Establishment

Bn HQ: (7)

HQ Coy: (156):

       Coy. HQ. (16)
       Admin. Pln. (39)
       QM Pln. (33)
       Signals Pln. (25)
       Tpt. Pln. (43)
       Med. Pln. (21)

2 Rifle Coys @ 140 each (280); 3rd rifle company on mobilization

       Coy. HQ (7)
       3 Plns. @ each 34 (102):
              Pln. HQ (4) *incl. one sniper*
              3 Secns. @ 10 each (30) ñ *1 x MAG*
       Weapons Pln. (31):
              Pln. HQ (3)
              Mortar Secn. (13) ñ *3 x 60 mm mrtrs.*
              A/T Secn. (9) ñ *3 x 84 mm RLs*
              MG Secn. (6) ñ *2 x 12.7 mm MGs*

Spt. Coy. (82):

       Coy. HQ (8)
       Mortar Pln. (28) ñ *4 x 81 mm mrtrs*
       A/T Pln. (23) ñ *4 x 90 mm RCLs*
       Recce Pln. (13)
       Assault Pioneer Pln. (10)

Total Peace establishment 546

Appendix IX: Irish Army Cavalry Squadron 1978 ñ Peacetime Establishment

HQ: (8) - *1 Land Rover & 4 Motorcycles*

      Admin Trp. (34) *ñ3 Land Rovers, 6 Trucks, 1 Tanker, 1 RV, 1 Workshop Vehicle*

3 Recce Trps. @ 26 each (78):
      Trp. HQ (3) ñ *1 x Land Rover*
      A/T Secn. (6) ñ *1 x Land Rover & 3 x 84 mm RCLs*
      Recce. Secn. (11) ñ *2 x Land Rovers*
      Lt. Armd. Car Secn. (6) ñ *2 x AML H-60s*

Spt. Trp. (39):

      Trp. HQ (3) ñ *1 x Land Rover*
      Hvy. Armd. Car Secn. (12) ñ *4 x AML H-90s*
      APC Secn. (24) ñ *3 x AML VTT M3 APCs*

Equipment: *4 x AML H-90s, 6 x AML H-60s, 3 x AML VTT M3s, 17 x Land Rovers, 6 x trucks, 1 x Recovery Vehicle, 1 x Workshop Vehicle & 4 motorcycles*

Total Peace Establishment: 159

Appendix X: Irish Army Artillery Regiment 1978 ñ Peacetime Establishment

RHQ (3)

HQ Bty (93)

       Bty HQ (7)
       Admin Trp. (8)
       QM Trp. (25)
       Signals Trp. (12)
       Tpt. Trp. (22)
       Survey Trp. (12)
       Intell./Mrtr. Locating Trp. (7)

Two Firing Batteries @ 82 each (164) Third battery on mobilization

       Bty. HQ (13)
       OP Grp. (5)
       Gun Grp. (64)

Total Peace establishment: 258

Appendix XI: Recommendations of the Efficiency Audit Group 1995

The Defence Forces Efficiency Audit Group examined three options for a one, two and three-brigade structure for the Irish Army. It concluded that the optimum would be a two-brigade force ñ one brigade with responsibility for the Border area and the other to cover the remainder of the country, except the Greater Dublin area which would be garrisoned by an independent battalion group with first call on the combat elements of the proposed National Training Centre (one Ranger company, one Light Tank squadron and an Air Defence Regiment). The composition of each Brigade was envisaged as follows:

HQ element	65
Three full-strength Infantry Battalions @ 540 each	1620
A Cavalry Squadron	100
An Artillery Regiment	225
An Engineer element	80
A Signals element	50
A Logistic Support element	100
A Medical Element	40
A Military Police element	30
TOTAL:	2310

The organization finally adopted envisaged a Brigade with a total of 2330 of which the infantry component would be three reduced infantry battalions of 470 each. (See Appendix XII below.)

Appendix XII: Current Irish Army Brigade Organization

The following Table shows the proposed composition of the PDF and Reserve Brigades as outlined in the Reserve Defences Forces Review Implementation Plan unveiled in July 2004. Some subsequent modifications will almost certainly be necessary.

RESERVE BRIGADE	ELEMENT	PDF BRIGADE (MOBILIZATION TO)	PDF BRIGADE (PEACE TO)	INTEGRATED RESERVE AUGMENTATION ELEMENT
58	Bde. HQ	70	67	3
37	Bde. Training Cntr	37	21	16
650	Infy. Bn. I	650	470	180
650	Infy. Bn. II	650	470	180
650	Infy. Bn. III	650	470	180
144	Cav. Sqn.	144	122	22
291	Arty. Rgt.	375	211	164
117	Engr. Coy.	117	88	29
71	CIS (Signals) Coy.	92	71	21
2668	COMBAT ELEMENTS	2785	1990	795
69	MP Coy	55	41	14
11	Logistics Bn. HQ	11	11	
66	Camp Staffs	111	111	
	Ord/Supply Coy.	43	43	
107	Transport Coy.	148	90	58
71	Medical Coy.	44	44	
324	SUPPORT ELEMENTS	412	340	72
2992	TOTAL	3197	2330	867

NOTES

(1) It appears that the establishment of the new Reserve Brigades and the mobilized PDF Brigades still differ in some detail and the following elements of both types of formation are not identical: Brigade HQ, Artillery Regiment, CIS Company, MP Company, Transport Company and Medical Company.

(2) The smaller Artillery element in the Reserve Brigade presumably reflects the absence of an integral air defence element ñ each type of unit contains three Field Artillery batteries, equipped with either the 105 mm Royal Ordnance Light Gun, the venerable Mk II 25 pounder gun-howitzer or the Brandt M50 120 mm mortar, on mobilization, but only the Regular Artillery Regiment includes an air-defence battery in its mobilization establishment

(3) The smaller CIS Company in the Reserve Brigade presumably reflects the relatively static defence role implicitly envisaged for these formations, as does the smaller Transport Company. Likewise, the larger Medical and Military Police Companies in the reserve formations reflect their probable inclusion of both a base hospital and a prison/internment camp element.

(4) The size of the Ordnance/Supply Company in the peacetime PDF Brigade seems extremely lean and would almost certainly be inadequate for operation in a wartime setting. The total lack of this element in the Reserve Brigade is even harder to understand but presumably reflects a political reluctance to transfer an excessive degree of know-how in the handling of explosives to the members of what remains a part-time force. Even accepting a relatively static defence role for each Reserve Brigade and their access to the logistic elements of the Defence Forces Logistic Base, such an element would be necessary for the effective functioning of each of the Reserve Brigades and will presumably be included in their final TO&E.

Appendix XIII: Break Down of Current Irish Army TOs (Notional)

1. INFANTRY BATTALION

<u>Regular Unit - Peacetime Establishment (470)</u>

Bn. HQ (11)

HQ Coy. (111)

       Coy. HQ (5)
       Admin. Pln. (11)
       Logs. Pln. (21)
       Tpt. Pln. (29)
       Wkshps. Pln. (9)
       CIS Pln. (21)
       Med. Pln. (15)

2 Infy. Coys @ 133 each (266)

       Coy HQ (7)
            3 Rifle Platoons @ 31 each (93):
                Pln. HQ (4) *incl one sniper*
                    3 Sections @ 9 *with one MAG 7.62mm and four AT-4 LAWs each* (27)

            Weapons Platoon (33)
                Pln. HQ (3)
                    MG Section (8) *with two Browning M2 HB 12.7 mm & two MAG 7.62 mm MGs*
                    Mortar Section (13) *with 3 Vektor 60 mm Mortars*
                    A/T Section (9) *with 3 Carl Gustav M 45 84 mm RCLs*

Support Coy (82)

            Coy HQ (5)
            Mortar Pln. (21) *with four Brandt 81 mm mortars*

      A/T pln. (21) *with four Milan or Javelin ATGWs plus four ART-4 LAWs*
            Assault Pioneer Pln. (21)
            Recce. Pln. (14) *with four AT-4 LAWs*

<u>Reserve Unit ñ Full Establishment/ Regular Unit - Mobilization Establishment (650)</u>

Bn. HQ (11)

HQ Coy. (111)

      Coy. HQ (5)
      Admin. Pln. (11)
      Logs. Pln. (21)
      Tpt. Pln. (29)
      Wkshps. Pln. (9)
      CIS Pln. (21)
      Med. Pln. (15)

3 Infy. Coys @ 143 each (399)

Coy HQ (7)

      3 Rifle Platoons @ 31 each (93):

            Pln. HQ (4) *incl one sniper*
            3 Sections @ 9 *with one MAG 7.62mm and four AT-4 LAWs each (27)*

      Weapons Platoon (43):

            Pln. HQ (3)
            MG Section (18) *4 Browning M2 HB 12.7 mm &4 MAG 7.62 mm MGs*
            Mortar Section (13) *with three Vektor 60 mm Mortars*
            A/T Section (9) *with 3 Carl Gustav M 45 84 mm RCLs*

Support Coy (119)

            Coy HQ (5)
            Mortar Pln. (31) *with six Brandt 81 mm mortars*
            A/T Pln. (31) *with six Milan or Javelin ATGWs plus four AT-4 LAWs*
                Assault Pioneer Pln. (31)
                Recce. Pln. (21) *with four AT-4 LAWs*

NOTE: The 12.7 mm HMG which was originally a battalion-level weapon seems to have been devolved downwards to the company-level weapons platoon

2. ARMOURED SQUADRON

Regular Unit ñ Peacetime Establishment (82):

> HQ (9) *with 2 Scorpion Lt. Tanks & 1 Nissan Patrol,*
> Admin Troop (25) 1 Nisssan Patrol, *7 trucks, 1 Recovery Vehicle & 1 Workshop Vehicle*
> 3 x Armd. Troops @ 16 *with 4 Scorpion Lt. Tanks & 1 Nissan Patrol each* (48)

Regular Unit ñ Mobilization Establishment (145):

> HQ (15) *with 1 Sultan Armoured Command Vehicle*, 2 Scorpion Lt. Tanks & 1 Nissan Patrol*
> Admin Troop (42) *with 3 Nissan Patrols, 6 Trucks, 1 Fuel Tanker, 1 Samson Armoured Recovery Vehicle* & 1 Workshop Vehicle, 1 tank transporter, 1 field Kitchen & 1 ambulance*
> 3 x Armd. Troops @ 16 *with 4 Scorpion Lt. Tanks & 1 Nissan Patrol each* (48)
> APC Troop (40) *with 3 Stormer APCs* & 1 Nissan Patrol*
>
> **To be acquired*

3. CAVALRY SQUADRON

Regular Unit - Peacetime Establishment (122):

> HQ (5) *with 1 Nissan Patrol & 2 motorcycles*
> Admin Troop (23) *with 1 Nissan Patrol, 7 Trucks, 1 Workshop Vehicle, 1 Recovery Vehicle*
> 3 x Recce. Troops @ 22 *with 2 AML H-20s + 3 Nissan Patrols & 1 Motorcycle each* (66)
> Support Troop (28) *with 3 AML H-90s, 2 TCVs & 1 Nissan Patrol*
>
> ** 2nd Cav. Sqn. also has 41 motorcycles for ceremonial purposes*

<u>Regular Unit - Mobilization Establishment</u> (144):

HQ (5) *with 1 Nissan Patrol & 2 motorcycles*
Admin Troop (29) *with 1 Nissan Patrol, 6 Trucks, 1 Fuel Tanker, 1 Workshop Vehicle, 1 Recovery Vehicle, 1 Field Kitchen, 1 Ambulance*
3 x Recce. Troops @ 22 *with 2 AML H-20s +3 Nissan Patrols & 1 Motorcycle each* (66)
Support Troop (44) *with 3 AML H-90s, 4 TCVs & 1 Nissan Patrol*

<u>Reserve Unit ñ Full Establishment</u> (144):

HQ (5) *with 1 Nissan Patrol & 2 motorcycles*
Admin Troop (29) *with 1 Nissan Patrol, 9 Trucks, 1 Workshop Vehicle, 1 Recovery Vehicle*
3 x Recce. Troops @ 22 *with 4 Nissan Patrols & 1 Motorcycle each* (66)
Support Troop (44) *with 3 AML H-90s, 4 TCVs & 1 Nissan Patrol*

4. ARTILLERY REGIMENT

<u>Regular Unit - Peacetime Establishment</u> (211):

RHQ (3)

HQ Bty (48)

Bty HQ (5)
Admin Trp. (6)
Logs. Trp. (11)
CIS Trp. (7)
Tpt. Trp. (14)
Med. Trp. (5)

2 Field Artillery Btys @ 80 each

Bty. HQ (5)
Survey Trp. (6)
Intell./Mrtr. Locating Trp. (7)
2 Gun Trps. @ 31 *with 3 x 105 mm light guns or 120 mm AM50 mortars each*

<u>Reserve Unit ñ Full Establishment</u> (291):

RHQ (3)

HQ Bty (48)

Bty HQ (5)
Admin Trp. (6)
Logs. Trp. (11)
CIS Trp. (7)
Tpt. Trp. (14)
Med. Trp. (5)

3 Field Artillery Btys @ 80 each (240)

Bty. HQ (5)
Survey Trp. (6)
Intell./Mrtr. Locating Trp. (7)
2 Gun Trps. @ 31 *with 3 x 25 pdr gun-howitzers or AM50 120 mm mortars each*

<u>Regular Unit - Mobilization Establishment</u> (375):

RHQ (3)

HQ Bty (48)

Bty HQ (5)
Admin Trp. (6)
Logs. Trp. (11)
CIS Trp. (7)
Tpt. Trp. (14)
Med. Trp. (5)

3 Field Artillery Btys @ 80 each (240)

Bty. HQ (5)
Survey Trp. (6)
Intell./Mrtr. Locating Trp. (7)
2 Gun Trps. @ 31 *with 3 x 105 mm light guns or AM50 120 mm mortars each*

Air Defence Bty. (84)

Bty. HQ (8)
2 Gun Trps. @ 38 *with 4 x 40 mm L/60 A/A guns each* (76)

NOTE: As the manpower establishment of the HQ Battery appears insufficient to accommodate the Survey Troop and the Intelligence/Mortar Location Troops it has been assumed that these have been assigned down to Firing Battery level and that an OP Group has been correspondingly assigned to each Gun Troop.

5. AIR DEFENCE REGIMENT

Combined Regular & Reserve Unit - Peacetime Establishment (243)

RHQ (3)

HQ Bty. (111)

Bty HQ (5)
Admin Trp. (11)
Logs. Trp. (21)
CIS Trp. (21)
Tpt. Trp. (29)
Wkshps. Trp. (9)
Med. Trp. (15)

1 (Regular) Bty. (129)

Bty. HQ (8)
Missile Trp. *with 6 x RBSwith70 SAM launchers + 1 Ericsson Giraffe Target Acquisition/Fire Control system* (45)
2 Gun Trps. @ 38 *with* 3 x 40 mm L/70 A/A guns + 1 Signaal Flycatcher *Target Acquisition/Fire Control system each* (76)

Mobilization Establishment (495)

RHQ (3)

HQ Bty. (111)

> Bty HQ (5)
> Admin Trp. (11)
> Logs. Trp. (21)
> CIS Trp. (21)
> Tpt. Trp. (29)

Wkshps. Trp. (9)
Med. Trp. (15)

1 (Regular) Bty. (129)

> Bty. HQ (8)
> Missile Trp. *with 6 x RBSwith70 SAM launchers + 1 Ericsson Giraffe Target Acquisition/Fire Control system* (45)
> 2 Gun Trps. @ 38 *with 3 x 40 mm L/70 A/A guns + 1 Signaal Flycatcher Target Acquisition/Fire Control system each* (76)

> 3 (Reserve) Btys *with @ 84 each (252)*

> Bty. HQ (8)
> 2 Gun Trps. @ 38 *with 3 x 40 mm L/70 A/A guns + 1 Signaal Flycatcher Target Acquisition/Fire Control system each* (76)

6. ENGINEER COMPANY

Regular Unit - Peacetime Establishment (88):

> HQ (9)
> 2 Sapper Plns @ 29 each (58)
> 1 Bridging Pln. (21)

Reserve Unit - Full Establishment/ Regular Unit - Mobilization Establishment (117):

> HQ (9)
> 3 Sapper Plns @ 29 each (87)
> 1 Bridging Pln. (21)

7.COMMUNICATIONS AND INFORMATION SYSTEMS COMPANY

Regular Unit - Peacetime Establishment (71):

> HQ (8)
> 2 CIS Plns. @ 21 each (42)
> 1 SIGINT Pln (21)

Reserve Unit - Full Establishment/ Regular Unit - Mobilization Establishment (92)

> HQ (8)
> 3 CIS Plns. @ 21 each (63)
> 1 SIGINT Pln. (21)

7. MP COMPANY

Regular Unit - Peacetime Establishment (41):

> HQ (5)
> Investigation Section (8)
> 2 Plns. @ 14 each (28)

Regular Unit - Mobilization Establishment (55):

> HQ (5)
> Investigation Section (8)
> 3 Plns. @ 14 each (42)

<u>Reserve Unit ñ Full Establishment</u> (69):

> HQ (5)
> Investigation Section (8)
> 4 Plns. @ 14 each (56)

8. LOGISTIC BATTALION

<u>Regular Unit - Peacetime Establishment</u> (188):

> Bn. HQ (11)
>
> Supply/Ordnance Coy. (43):
>
>> HQ (8)
>> Supply Pln. (21)
>> Ordn. Pln. (14)
>
> Transport Company (90):
>
>> HQ (11)
>> 2 Tpt. Plns. @ 29 each (58)
>> Recovery & Workshop Pln. (21)
>
> Medical Company (44):
>
>> HQ (5)
>> 2 Casevac Plns. @ 15 each (30)
>> 1 Dressing Station (9)

<u>Reserve Unit ñ Full Establishment</u> (231):

> Bn. HQ (11)
>
> Supply/Ordnance Coy. (43):
>
>> HQ (8)
>> Supply Pln. (21)
>> Ordn. Pln. (14)

Transport Company (107):

HQ (6)
3 Tpt. Plns. @ 29 each (87)
Recovery & Workshop Pln. (14)

Medical Company (71):

HQ (5)
3 Casevac. Plns. & 15 each (45)
1 Field Hospital (21)

Regular Unit - Mobilization Establishment (246):

Bn. HQ (11)

Supply/Ordnance Coy. (43):

HQ (8)
Supply Pln. (21)
Ordn. Pln. (14)

Transport Company (148):

HQ (11)
4 Tpt. Plns. @ 29 each (116)
Recovery & Workshop Pln. (21)

Medical Company (44):

HQ (5)
2 Casevac. Plns. @ 15 each (30)
1 Dressing Station (9)

All of the above details are based on incomplete information and represent an educated
ì guesstimateî based on known global figures for each element down to Company level in
the context of known details of the previously existing

Select Bibliography

The following works were consulted in the preparation of this study. The list should not be taken as a comprehensive bibliography of the subject. Some of the titles are misleading, e.g. the first item ì AIR RAID MESSAGE REDî deals with the current organization and equipment of the Air Defence Regiment; ì TOUGH AT THE BOTTOMî is an insight-full account of soldiering in the 1950s and provides the surprising information, inter alia, that the 13th Infantry Battalion had four rather than the usual two rifle companies for at least part of that period. Although a number of the works cited in the following list are primarily pictorial they frequently contain useful information regarding the location of units and their equipment at various times.

Bourke, Wesley. AIR RAID MESSAGE RED. An CosantÛr, The Irish Defence
    Journal, Vol. 64, No. 7. September 2004

THE CALL TO ARMS   No Publisher, No Date

Carroll, J.T. IRELAND IN THE WAR YEARS, 1939-45David & Charles, Newton
    Abbot, UK 1975

Conway, NoÎl THE BLOODS, Officersí Association 3rd Battalion, The Curragh, 1973

Daly, P.J., Lt. Col. THE VOLUNTEER FORCE, An CosantÛr, The Irish Defence
    Journal, Vol.XXXVIII, No. 2, Dublin 1978.

DEFENCE FORCES ANNUAL REPORT 2000, Defence Forces Printing Press,
    Dublin July 2001

DEFENCE FORCES ANNUAL REPORT 2002, Defence Forces Printing Press,
    Dublin July 2003

DEFENCE FORCES ANNUAL REPORT 2003, Defence Forces Printing Press,
    Dublin July 2004

DEFENCE FORCES HANDBOOK 1968, An CosantÛr, Dublin 1968

DEFENCE FORCES HANDBOOK 1974, An CosantÛr, Dublin 1974

DEFENCE FORCES HANDBOOK 1982, An CosantÛr, Dublin, 1982

DEFENCE FORCES HANDBOOK 1988, An CosantÛr, Dublin, 1988

THE DEFENCE FORCES IN FOCUS. Defence Forces PR Section, 1999

THE DEFENCE FORCES IN FOCUS. (Second Edition) Defence Forces PR Section,
    2002

DEFENCE FORCES TODAY. An CosantÛr, The Irish Defence Journal,
    Vol.XXXVII, No. 1, Dublin 1977,

DEFENDING THE FUTURE ñ Defence White Paper Submission by the
    Representative Association of Commissioned Officers, Dublin. No date

Duggan, J.P. Lt. THE ARTILLERY CORPS, An CosantÛr, The Irish Defence Journal,
    Vol. II, No. 2. Dublin 1947

Duggan, J.P., Lt. Col (retd.) A HISTORY OF THE IRISH ARMY, Gill & Macmillan,
    Dublin 1991

English, A.J. REPUBLIC OF IRELANDíS DEFENCE FORCES. Janeís Defence
    Review, Vol. 2, No. 4, 1981 Janeís Publishing Company, London 1981

English, A.J. THE IRISH REPUBLIC - ODD MAN OUT IN EUROPEAN
DEFENCE. Janeís Military Review 1987 Janeís Publishing Company,
London, 1987

Fisk, Robert. IN TIME OF WAR AndrÈ Deutsch, London 1983.

FitzGerald, Captain Fergus. IRISH MECHANIZED CAVALRY DURING WORLD
WAR II PERIOD. An CosantÛr, The Irish Defence Journal, Vol VII, No. 6.
Dublin 1947.

IN THE SERVICE OF PEACE. (Editor Commandant Brendan OíShea). An CosantÛr,
Dublin, 2001

IRISH ARMY PICTORIAL. No Publisher. No date.

IRISH BATT. 66th IRISH BATTALION UNIFIL, OCTOBER 1989 ñ APRIL 1990.
An CosantÛr, The Irish Defence Journal. Special Issue

THE IRISH DEFENCE FORCES AND THE UNITED NATIONS. The Irish Sword
Vol. XX, No.79. Military History Society of Ireland, Dublin 1993-94

Keegan, John, WORLD ARMIES. Macmillan, London. 1st Edition 1979. 2nd Edition
1983.

LAUNCH OF THE RESERVE DEFENCE FORCE REVIEW IMPLEMENTATION
PLAN. Defence Forces Printing Press, Dublin July 2004

LOCATION OF UNITS IN THE DEFENCE FORCES. An CosantÛr, The Irish Defence
Journal, Vol. XXXVIII, No. 1, Dublin 1978

Mc Carthy, Denis J. ARMOURED FIGHTING VEHICLES OF THE ARMY No. 10
Universal Carriers. An CosantÛr, The Irish Defence Journal, Vol. XLI, No. 11, Dublin
November 1981

Mc Carthy, Denis J. ARMOURED FIGHTING VEHICLES OF THE ARMY No. 12
Beaverette Armoured Cars. An CosantÛr, The Irish Defence Journal, Vol. XLII, No. 1,
January 1982

THE NATION IS PROFOUNDLY GRATEFUL. The Irish Defence Forces 1939-46.
Military Archives, Dublin. 1996

G. OíBrien, Captain. A NEW DEPARTURE IN IRISH PEACE-KEEPING. An
CosantÛr, The Irish Defence Journal, Vol. 63, No. 10, December-January 2004

W. OíDwyer, Commandant. SUPPORT IN THE FIELD. An CosantÛr, The Irish
Defence Journal, Vol. 64, No. 5. July-August 2004

RESERVE DEFENCE FORCE REVIEW IMPLEMENTATION PLAN. An CosantÛr,
The Irish Defence Journal, Special Supplement, September 2004.

SPECIAL OPERATIONS TASK GROUP LIBERIA. An CosantÛr, The Irish Defence
Journal, Vol. 64, No. 1, March 2004.

THE EMERGENCY 1939-45. The Irish Sword Vol XIX, Nos. 75 & 76. Military History
Society of Ireland, Dublin 1993-94

Keatinge, Patrick. A SINGULAR STANCE. Institute of Public Administration, Dublin,
1984

Mac Carron, Donal, STEP TOGETHER, IRELANDíS EMERGENCY ARMY 1939-46.
Irish Academic Press, Dublin 1999

Martin, Karl, IRISH ARMY VEHICLES, Published by the author, Dublin 2002

THE MILITARY BALANCE. International Institute for Strategic Studies, London, Annual 1973 onwards

Moriarity, M., Lt. Col. AM 50 (120 mm MORTAR) ñ Artillery Workhorse, An CosantÛr, The Irish Defence Journal, Vol.XLI, No. 9, Dublin 1981.

Morrison, George. THE IRISH CIVIL WAR ñ AN ILLUSTRATED HISTORY. Gill & Macmillan, Dublin 1981

Neeson, Eoin. THE CIVIL WAR IN IRELAND .Poolbeg Press, Dublin, 1989.

OíFarrell, Mick. TOUGH AT THE BOTTOM. Arriba Publications, Dublin 1999.

REVIEW OF THE DEFENCE FORCES, Department of Defence 1995

Share, Bernard. THE EMERGENCY. Gill & Macmillan, Dublin, 1978.

Smith, Raymond UNDER THE BLUE FLAG, Aherlow Publishers, Dublin, 1980

25th ANNIVERSARY OF THE 1ST TANK SQUADRON. Special Edition of An CosantÛr, The Irish Defence Journal, Vol.XLV, No. 1, Dublin, January 1985.

U.N. ANNIVERSARY EDITION of An CosantÛr, The Irish Defence Journal, Vol. LV,, No. 7. Dublin October 1995.

Von Pifka, Otto. THE ARMIES OF EUROPE TODAY, Osprey Publishing Co., Reading U.K., 1974

Weeks, John. JANEíS POCKET BOOK: ARMIES OF THE WORLD. Janeís Publishing Company, London 1981

WHITE PAPER ON DEFENCE, Government Publications Sales Office, Dublin 2000

WORLD ARMIES (Editor Chris Westhorpe). Salamander Books, London, 1991

Younger, Calton. IRELANDíS CIVIL WAR. Frederick M ̦ller 1968.

The Author

Adrian J. English was born in Tipperary, Ireland and qualified as an architect in 1964. In the early 1970s, whilst still working as an architect, he began writing about military and defence matters, in which he has had a life-long interest, and has since published many articles and several books, mainly about Latin America, where he has travelled extensively. A first visit to Sweden in 1994 re-awakened a dormant interest in Swedish defence. Several subsequent visits led to a book slated for publication in 2005. Living in Ireland, he also has an abiding interest in Irish defence, which is only matched by a profound contempt for what he regards as his country's hypocritical pretence of neutrality.

www.ingramcontent.com/pod-product-compliance
Lightning Source LLC
Chambersburg PA
CBHW062045090426
42740CB00016B/3024